P9-CKD-546

THE
MONKEY
TRIAL

chez, Anita, 1956-
Monkey Trial : John
es and the battle over tea

5254044450
05/26/23

THE
MONKEY
TRIAL

JOHN SCOPES AND THE BATTLE
OVER TEACHING EVOLUTION

By Anita Sanchez

Clarion Books
An Imprint of HarperCollinsPublishers

Clarion Books is an imprint of HarperCollins Publishers.

The Monkey Trial
Copyright © 2023 by Anita Sanchez
All rights reserved. Printed in the United States of America.
No part of this book may be used or reproduced in any manner
whatsoever without written permission except in the case of
brief quotations embodied in critical articles and reviews. For
information address HarperCollins Children's Books, a division of
HarperCollins Publishers, 195 Broadway, New York, NY 10007.
www.harpercollinschildrens.com

ISBN 978-0-35-845769-5

Typography by Anthony Elder
23 24 25 26 27 LBC 5 4 3 2 1

First Edition

This is for Alex

Contents

Introduction

"Call Howard Morgan to the Stand"

FOURTEEN-YEAR-OLD Howard Morgan was not used to wearing a tie. That morning, he had struggled in front of the bathroom mirror to get the thin strand knotted properly under his stiff collar. Now, as he walked to the front of the courtroom, the tie had slewed around until it was almost under one ear. Too late to fix it. The Rhea County Courthouse was jammed with hundreds of spectators—standing room only— and every eye was aimed at him.

Everyone in the courthouse was dripping with sweat. The July afternoon was hot and humid, and the temperature in the building was well over ninety degrees. Howard took his seat on the carved wooden chair high on a platform and clutched the armrests.

The judge and a dozen lawyers clustered at the front of the packed courtroom. Most of the lawyers were strangers to Howard, but he recognized William Jennings Bryan, one of the most famous men in America. Howard had seen his picture often enough in the papers, since Bryan had run for president three times. Mr. Bryan was waving a palm-leaf fan in front of his face, which was red with heat. Howard also recognized the defense lawyer, Clarence Darrow. Mr. Darrow, like most of the lawyers, had removed his jacket because of the sweltering temperature, and he grinned as he flaunted bright purple suspenders. And Mr. Scopes, one of Howard's favorite teachers at the high school, was there in the front of the room, sitting at a long table and watching quietly.

A shiny microphone was just inches away from Howard's seat on the witness platform. Wires snaked through the courthouse, winding along the floor and dangling from the rafters. Radio announcers and reporters were waiting eagerly to hear what he would say. Howard fidgeted on the hard wooden seat as Tom Stewart, the prosecutor, approached.

The first question was easy:

Your name is Howard Morgan?

Howard answered in a clear, high-pitched voice:

Yes, sir.

You are Mr. Luke Morgan's son?

Yes, sir.

Your father is in the bank here, Dayton Bank and Trust company?

Yes, sir.

The prosecutor held up a scuffed green-covered book Howard recognized: Hunter's *Civic Biology.*

Were you studying that book in April of this year, Howard?

Yes, sir.

Did Professor Scopes teach it to you?

Howard replied in almost a whisper. *Yes, sir.*

Then came the all-important question, the one Howard was waiting for. *State in your own words, Howard, what he taught you.*

Howard knew the answer, almost as well as he knew his own name. He had rehearsed it often enough. Mr. Scopes himself had coached him thoroughly, preparing him for this cross-examination as though it were just another biology test.

Howard took a deep breath and spoke clearly. "He said that the earth was once a hot molten mass too hot for plant or animal life to exist upon it; in the sea the earth cooled off; there was a little germ of one-cell organism formed, and this organism kept evolving until it got to be a pretty good-sized animal, and then came on to be a land animal and it kept on evolving, and from this was man."

The prosecutor gave a satisfied nod. Howard's

Howard Morgan was an eyewitness to the crime.

testimony had removed all doubt—he was an eyewitness. Mr. Scopes had committed the crime of teaching Darwin's theory of evolution in the classroom of a Tennessee public school.

Chapter One

"John, Would You Be Willing to Stand for a Test Case?"

THREE MONTHS BEFORE the trial that would bitterly divide the nation, a group of students took their seats in Mr. Scopes's classroom. They expected that this would be just another high school biology class. No one had any idea that this spring day would go down in history.

Dayton, Tennessee, was a quiet town of comfortable homes on tree-lined streets. Rhea Central High School was one of the county's newest buildings, a two-story square of brick on the edge of town, surrounded by rolling hills and farmland. It was a pleasant morning in April 1925, the weather already warm and humid as the school day began. The students sat in rows at their wooden desks in a stuffy classroom. The teacher, a young man with spectacles and sandy hair, took his place in front of the room as the students obediently opened their textbooks to review for their upcoming biology exam. But no one was paying much attention as he began to read. After all, their regular teacher was out for the day. Mr. Scopes was just a sub.

John Scopes was a popular teacher and coached the Dayton high school football team to the playoffs.

John Scopes was a newcomer—he had lived in Dayton for less than a year. So far he had only taught physics, as well as being a part-time coach. He was younger than the other teachers, only twenty-four, so he could run around on the football field as fast as the high school athletes he was coaching. A small, slender man, he was often described as quiet and unassuming.

Howard Morgan, senior Bud Shelton, and other students sat at their desks, listening (or not) as their teacher droned on. But what did John Scopes teach on that sleepy spring morning that got him arrested, launched him into international fame, and forever changed his life?

Later, no one could remember exactly what the lesson involved—not the students, not Mr. Scopes himself.

Even the exact date was debated—some said April 21 and others remembered it as April 23. All they knew was that he had read to them out of their usual textbook. Hunter's *Civic Biology* had a section on evolution, which explained what Howard later testified in court— that humans had evolved from one-celled organisms.

The concept of evolution was often referred to as Darwinism after Charles Darwin, a British scientist who had died almost fifty years earlier. Darwin had spent decades formulating his Theory of Evolution: that all living things had developed, over immense periods of time, from simpler life-forms. Darwin included people in his theory, explaining that humans had evolved from the same family tree as apes.

Darwin's book *On the Origin of Species* was an immediate bestseller when it was published in 1859. His work gave scientists a whole new way to study living organisms and became the basis of modern biology. But many devout Christians were deeply disturbed by Darwin's ideas. Evolution seemed to contradict the Bible, which described how God had miraculously created all living things in six days.

Some Christians felt that the biblical account meant that all species were perfect as God first created them, so that while a species might go extinct, it could never change. Therefore, new species could not evolve. And, according to the Bible, "man" was a special being, placed by God in charge of all other life on earth. But Darwin's theory of evolution meant that humans were

WHAT IS
EVOLUTION?

CHARLES DARWIN was a nineteenth-century British scientist who spent decades carefully observing plants and animals to develop his Theory of Evolution. He described the concept of natural selection, in which traits that help an organism survive may be passed down to its young. For example, as he studied finches, he noticed that species of these small birds looked very similar— except for differently shaped beaks.

Darwin wondered if all these types of finches might once have been a single species that had split into several different species. (A species is a population of animals that does not usually interbreed and cannot produce fertile young.)

Let's say a particular finch has an extra-strong beak that lets it crack hard-shelled seeds. This bird would be able to get more food than other finches, and so would likely survive better and produce more babies. And some of the young birds might inherit that strong beak. Meanwhile, finches that have differently shaped beaks might be better at sipping nectar, or catching insects. After long ages of time, one species of finch could evolve into different species.

1. Geospiza magnirostris.
3. Geospiza parvula.
2. Geospiza fortis.
4. Certhidea olivasea.

just one species out of millions.

At first, interest in this complex topic was mostly confined to scientists, college professors, and members of the clergy. There wasn't a lot of controversy over whether to teach Darwinism in American high schools— because there *weren't* many high schools. In the early 1900s, almost all students in the United States finished their education by the fifth or sixth grade. But in the rush of prosperity after the end of World War I, communities began to fund public high schools. In Tennessee, as in all southern states, schools were segregated by law, and there were only a few high schools for Black students. But by 1925, most high schools for white students, like the one in Dayton, were beginning to teach sciences: chemistry, physics, biology.

As more students started coming home from school with new ideas of science, some parents got worried. If youngsters began to question the Bible, where would it stop? Fundamentalist Christians began a national crusade to oust Charles Darwin's theories from America's classrooms. Soon, a dozen states were considering anti-evolution legislation.

In January of 1925, John Butler, a devout Christian member of the Tennessee state legislature, proposed a bill that would make it illegal to "teach any theory that denies the story of the Divine Creation of man as taught in the Bible."

While state senators debated the Butler Act, the citizens of Tennessee weighed in. Letters criticizing or praising the new law appeared in newspapers. Sermons were preached both for and against it. The bill was signed into law by the governor on March 21, 1925.

However, the Butler Act hadn't generated a huge amount of publicity. *Evolution* was not yet a household word across America, not even in Tennessee. The Butler Act was only a month old when Mr. Scopes read aloud from *Civic Biology* on that April morning. At the time, none of the students noticed anything out of the ordinary—there were no raised eyebrows, no gasps of horror. After school, the Dayton students went home and forgot about Mr. Scopes's lesson. So did John Scopes.

It wasn't until a few weeks later, in early May, that he received a message urging him to hurry over to Robinson's Drug Store, where a group of local business owners were about to ask him the most important question of his life.

SCHOOL WAS OUT, and it was time to play. John Scopes was enjoying the early start of summer vacation—schools in rural areas often closed at the end of April so that kids who lived on farms could help with the spring chores. He was relaxing as he often did, by challenging a couple of his students to a brisk game of tennis.

They were volleying back and forth on a weedy clay court at the town park. The morning sun was hot, and they'd worked up a good sweat. But the game was abruptly interrupted by a boy, who called, "Mr. Scopes?

Automobiles were replacing horses on Dayton's streets.

Mr. Robinson says, if it's convenient, for you to come down to the drugstore."

The message didn't sound very urgent, so John took time to finish the tennis game. Then he strolled into town, wondering what on earth it was all about.

It was a short, pleasant walk along shady streets. Most Dayton roads were still dirt lanes, although Main Street had recently been paved. Many of the citizens had given up horse-drawn buggies and learned to drive cars, and the town speed limit was twelve miles per hour.

There were more than a dozen churches, and most Daytonites went to church every Sunday, including John Scopes. Dayton was the local shopping headquarters for Rhea County, and John walked past feed stores and hardware stores as well as a movie theater and a big hotel.

But not all was well with Dayton. It was a place that was shrinking, not growing. The town had once been a thriving commercial center, powered by coal mines and an iron industry. But a series of accidents and explosions had crippled the mines and shut down most of the factories. The

Churches were a major part of social life in Dayton. John Scopes loved church picnics and ice cream socials.

population was dwindling as young people left to find jobs in larger cities. Stores, hotels, and other businesses were struggling. The economy of Dayton was in trouble.

And a young, hustling businessman named George Rappleyea was determined to do something about it.

Earlier that May morning, Rappleyea had read an article in the local paper that gave him an intriguing idea. He hurried downtown to talk with other businessmen at their usual meeting place: F. E. Robinson's Drug Store.

Doc Robinson's store was much more than a

Doc Robinson's drugstore was Dayton's unofficial town hall.

pharmacy. In addition to aspirin, Pepto-Bismol, and other remedies, Robinson's sold newspapers, books, candy bars, and just about everything else. Like most drugstores in those days, it was also a restaurant, a teen hangout, and ladies' social club. Small tables dotted the store where customers could enjoy an ice cream sundae or a Coca-Cola. The town's leaders met there to discuss important issues over sodas and cigarettes (smoking was legal everywhere, and most men smoked cigarettes or pipes).

There would later be several versions of how the famous "Monkey Trial" got started. Rappleyea and others would often reenact their historic meeting in the drugstore, posing for commemorative photographs. As the drugstore owner remembered, George Rappleyea burst into the store waving a newspaper and said, "Mr. Robinson, you . . . are always looking for something that will get Dayton a little publicity. I wonder if you have seen the morning paper?" He pointed to an article stating that the American Civil Liberties Union (ACLU) would pay the expenses of any teacher willing to challenge the new anti-evolution law.

The ACLU was a not-for-profit organization formed to defend the rights guaranteed to United States citizens by the Constitution. They saw the Butler Act as a threat to one of the most cherished rights of Americans: freedom of speech. But to challenge the anti-evolution law, the ACLU lawyers first needed someone to break it. Newspapers across the country carried the article saying the organization was looking for a teacher who would be willing to serve as a test case.

"Distinguished counsel [lawyers] have volunteered their services," Rappleyea read out loud. "All we need now is a willing client."

Like many citizens of Dayton, George Rappleyea wasn't in favor of the anti-evolution law—in fact, he had written to the newspapers protesting it. But he also saw a golden opportunity to focus a national spotlight on his town. He realized that a trial on this explosive issue could put Dayton on the map. Not to mention that it would bring in business! Tourists, he hoped, would flock to Dayton to see the trial and spend money in hotels, stores, and restaurants.

Walter White, the school superintendent, stopped by the drugstore for a soda. He was quickly converted to the idea, as were two local lawyers. Then one of the lawyers, Sue Hicks (his unusual name came from his mother), suggested they talk with his friend John Scopes, who was a science teacher.

When John arrived at the drugstore, the group sat down at one of the little round tables in back. Scents of mint and chocolate drifted agreeably from the nearby soda fountain. Hot and thirsty, John was thoughtfully provided with a free soda by Doc Robinson.

"John, we've been arguing," George Rappleyea told him. "And I said that nobody could teach biology without teaching evolution."

"That's right," the teacher agreed, sipping his soda

The original group that planned the arrest met several times to take carefully staged photographs recreating the event. Actually, John had just come from a sweaty game of tennis, and everyone was most likely smoking and sipping sodas.

and wondering where this was leading. He grabbed a textbook off a nearby shelf (Robinson's sold textbooks as well as everything else). Opening to the pages that explained evolution, he showed it to the assembled men.

"You've been teaching 'em this book?" George Rappleyea asked, making sure of the facts. Scopes nodded.

"Then you've been violating the law!" Rappleyea exclaimed triumphantly, handing John the newspaper article. Then he asked, "John, would you be willing to stand for a test case?"

Suddenly, John Scopes was faced with a life-changing decision. If he said yes, he would immediately be arrested. While he probably wouldn't spend time in

HUNTER'S *CIVIC BIOLOGY*

—•—

The Doctrine of Evolution.—We have now learned that animal forms may be arranged so as to begin with very simple one-celled forms and culminate with a group which contains man himself. This arrangement is called the evolutionary series. Evolution means change, and these groups are believed by scientists to represent stages in complexity of development of life on the earth. Geology teaches that millions of years ago, life upon the earth was very simple, and that gradually more and more complex forms of life appeared, as the rocks formed latest in time show the most highly developed forms of animal life. The great English scientist, Charles Darwin, from this and other evidence, explained the theory of evolution. This is the belief that simple forms of life on the earth slowly and gradually gave rise to those more complex and that thus ultimately the most complex forms came into existence.

jail, the arrest would be on his record for the rest of his life. He would be viewed with suspicion or disgust by his church-going neighbors. He'd probably lose his job. Worst of all, there would be publicity, something the shy, quiet man despised.

But at stake was something John believed in very deeply: the rights of his students to study whatever they wanted to, and to make their own decisions about what they believed.

Eagerly, the group of businessmen around the drug-store table waited for his answer.

Chapter Two

"We've Just Arrested a Man for Teaching Evolution!"

JOHN SCOPES WAS arrested for teaching evolution on May 5, 1925, but he wasn't handcuffed and thrown in jail. He wasn't marched off to stand before a judge. When he agreed to plead guilty to the offense of teaching evolution, nothing about his life changed—at least, not right away. After being informed by a hastily summoned constable that he was officially under arrest, John was allowed to finish his soda and go back to the tennis court for another game. But his quiet answer had set powerful forces in motion, like the tiny pebble that starts an avalanche.

The enterprising group of businessmen immediately

started spreading the word. George Rappleyea raced off to send a telegram to the ACLU informing them that Dayton had a teacher willing to stand trial. Meanwhile, Fred Robinson, delighted by the success of the idea that had been born in his drugstore, dashed to the telephone and called a local newspaper, the *Chattanooga News*. "This is F. E. Robinson in Dayton," he announced. "I'm a chairman of the school board here. We've just arrested a man for teaching evolution." Superintendent White contacted a reporter he knew from Nashville. News was spreading fast.

Next morning, "Arrest Under Evolution Law" was a front-page headline in the *Nashville Banner*. The *Chattanooga News* had an article about the arrest as well. The Associated Press, a national news organization, picked it up, and articles started appearing in major cities across the country. Overnight, the "Scopes affair" was national news.

Soon the name John Scopes would be famous all around the globe—which John began to realize with dread.

What was it that prompted this quiet, ordinary person to step up and get involved? In later years, John Scopes remembered that it was the thought of his father that gave him courage to take a stand. "I had been taught from childhood to stand up for what I thought was right," John wrote. "I did not think the state of Tennessee had any right to keep me from teaching the truth."

Thomas Scopes, John's father, had immigrated to America in the late 1800s. Born in the slums of London, England, he was a laborer with no family or wealth, but unlike many working-class people of his day, he could read. And Thomas loved to read. When he stepped off the boat in his new country, Thomas had almost nothing in his suitcase except books, including the Holy Bible and Darwin's *Origin of Species*.

Thomas got a job working as a railway machinist, and later became an activist for the rights of working people, organizing labor unions. John was the fifth child of Thomas and his wife, Emily, and he grew up in a household that valued books, discussion, and activism to protect the rights of others. He remembered his father reading aloud to him and his sisters from a wide array of books, including ones by Charles Darwin.

John went to high school in Salem, Illinois. It was a quiet town, as small and unexciting as Dayton, famous for just one thing—being the birthplace of a national superstar, a politician and orator named William Jennings Bryan.

John Scopes was in the class of 1919 at Salem High School. When it was time for that year's graduation ceremonies, the citizens of Salem felt fortunate to have their famous hometown son give the commencement address. William Jennings Bryan was revered across the country as a fierce defender of the rights of the "common working man." He had run for president

William Jennings Bryan had been a

force in American politics for decades, starting with his run for the presidency in 1896. He served as secretary of state under President Woodrow Wilson, but resigned in protest when Wilson led America into World War I. Bryan was a liberal crusader who was passionate about defending the rights of "the common man," and was nicknamed "The Great Commoner." And he defended the rights of women, too, as he was an early supporter of women's right to vote.

three times, and come very close to winning. His fierce speeches in defense of struggling farmers and labor unions battling for fair pay and safe working conditions made him immensely popular.

William Jennings Bryan was famous for his dramatic and powerful speeches, delivered in a deep, ringing voice.

Dressed in cap and gown, John sat with his fellow seniors, listening to Bryan's speech. But as Bryan reached the peak of his inspirational lecture, he accidentally made a funny whistling sound as he pronounced a word. Scopes and his friends tried to keep straight faces, but they couldn't help erupting in laughter. The thread of the speech was broken, the audience distracted.

Perhaps no one had ever giggled at William Jennings Bryan before. Visibly upset, he glared at the seniors as a smothered wave of laughter rippled through the audience. Bryan kept an angry eye on John and the others through the rest of the speech, as though memorizing their faces.

John soon forgot all about the incident as he headed off to college. He never imagined that he and Bryan would meet again.

At the University of Kentucky, John majored in law,

but after graduation he couldn't decide what he wanted to do. Drifting by chance to the small town of Dayton, he got a job filling in for a teacher who had quit unexpectedly. John was delighted to be earning such a nice paycheck: thirty-seven dollars a week! And he liked his new job, especially the fun of coaching the football team. Dayton had been a quiet, friendly, easygoing place to live—until now.

For a few days, John went about his usual business, uneasily aware of the suspicious glances of his neighbors. But nothing unusual happened until the morning a ragged-looking stranger walked up to him, stuck out his hand to shake, and said, "Boy, I'm interested in your case."

The stranger was an elderly man, wearing a suit of clothes that looked as though he slept in them. Scraggly gray hair hung on his forehead, and he needed a shave. But his piercing eyes showed a "keen and analytical mind," Scopes noticed. John Neal was a law professor who believed profoundly in academic freedom, and he had traveled to Dayton to volunteer to defend Scopes. "And whether you want me or not, I'm going to be here!" he assured the surprised teacher.

Neal had been recently fired from the University of Tennessee. He believed it was because he used a textbook that discussed evolution, but school officials claimed it was on account of his unusual teaching techniques. Instead of lecturing, Neal discussed current events, asked students for their opinions, and rarely

John Neal (left) was the first lawyer to jump into the Scopes case—but not the last.

bothered to grade exams. Scopes took to Neal at once, calling him "one of the warmest-hearted men I have ever known." Neal represented Scopes at a preliminary hearing on May 9, when the teacher's case was referred to a grand jury that would meet later in the summer.

But John Neal wasn't the only lawyer interested in the Scopes case. His abrupt arrival was just the beginning of an invasion of out-of-towners. The ACLU was rounding up a whole team of top-notch lawyers to defend Scopes. And two weeks after his arrest, John Scopes was staggered to hear the news that a very high-powered lawyer indeed had volunteered—but not for his defense. John Scopes was going to be prosecuted by a man he remembered all too well as being a brilliant orator: William Jennings Bryan.

BRYAN HAD GIVEN his immense influence and popularity to aid many different causes, but by 1925, he had narrowed his efforts to a single goal: to ban Darwin from America's classrooms. But why had evolution become such a hot topic?

The "Roaring Twenties" was a time of change in America—and change can be frightening. More and more young people were heading to the cities for jobs instead of staying in the small towns where they had grown up. Girls were wearing shorter skirts, almost up to the knee! Jazz music, movies, votes for women—the world was changing, fast. And, many parents feared, youngsters were drifting away from religion.

Bryan had become a leader among Fundamentalist Christians, many of whom believed that the Bible should be taken literally. Some Fundamentalists had a deep-rooted mistrust of science. Darwinism was (and is to this day) despised by many Christian Fundamentalists, and they were the driving force in getting anti-evolution laws into state legislatures. Tennessee had been their first big success, and they predicted that the

✷ The Battle Hymn of ✷
TENNESSEE

MRS. E. P. BLAIR • NASHVILLE TENNESSEAN, JUNE 29, 1925

★★★

Between Truth and Error, Right and Wrong,
The fight is on.
For country, God, and mother's song
It must be won!
Go sound the alarm, go gather your forces,
Oh Tennessee!
Land of the pioneer, home of the volunteer,
The daring, the free . . .

Now Error, the monster, calls forth her cohorts
From sea to sea.
They come from earth's four corners down
To Tennessee.
They challenge your power to rule your own
Your rights deny.
They scoff at you, ridicule you
Your laws defy.

Their forces are clad in garments great
Of science and law.
With the camouflage cloak of knowledge
To hide their claw.
So look at the havoc and heartache of nations
Where they have passed through.
Their blasting breath has meant instant death
To the noble and true.

Butler Act was the beginning of a wave of anti-evolution legislation that would sweep the country.

Bryan's public announcement that he would serve without pay as a special prosecutor for the state of Tennessee created a tidal wave of national headlines. His star power guaranteed that the eyes of the world would soon be turned on the Rhea County Courthouse.

And the Scopes trial was shaping up to be well worth watching. Across the nation, all sorts of people—lawyers, preachers, teachers, reporters, salesmen—were eager to get in on the action. That hot and humid spring, as John Scopes bitterly remarked, "the circus came to Dayton!"

MEDIA IN THE SPOTLIGHT:

𝕹𝖊𝖜𝖘𝖕𝖆𝖕𝖊𝖗𝖘

IN 1925, MOST PEOPLE GOT THEIR NEWS THE OLD-FASHIONED WAY: FROM A NEWSPAPER.

Newspapers have been around since the invention of the printing press in the fifteenth century, and even before the American Revolution, Benjamin Franklin was publishing one of America's first newspapers.

Especially in rural regions with little radio access, people relied on the papers for news of their neighborhood, their town, and the larger world beyond. There were thousands of small-town papers like the *Chattanooga News* and the *Nashville Tennessean*. These local newspapers served as today's Craigslist, eBay, Facebook, and Twitter. If you gave a party, the society page would report what kind of refreshments you made. If you wanted to buy a car, get a job, or discover what your favorite movie star was up to, you could find it in the newspaper.

The big-city papers, like the *New York Times* and the *Chicago Sun*, kept people up to date on national and international news. And like the TV news stations of today, each newspaper had its own particular slant: conservative, liberal, or in-between.

THE BLACK PRESS

In the South of the 1920s, every aspect of life was segregated. Black and white readers often read different newspapers. The Scopes trial was an issue of special interest to Black readers. An editorial in the *Chicago Defender*, one of the main African-American newspapers in the country, stated, "The Tennessee legislators who passed the law . . . probably have never read the text themselves and all they know about the subject is that the entire human race is supposed to have started from a common origin. Therein lies their difficulty."

Slave owners for centuries had used the Bible to justify enslaving other humans. Some Christians interpreted the Bible to imply that one of Noah's sons, who had been accursed for committing a crime, was the ancestor of all dark-skinned races. But the science of evolution meant that humans of all races had developed from the same source: Darwin's "one-celled organism."

IN THE SOUTH OF THE 1920s, EVERY ASPECT OF LIFE WAS SEGREGATED.

While white newspaper writers often found comedy and poked fun at the goings-on in Dayton, Black journalists tended to view the Scopes trial more seriously, deeply concerned about a law against the freedom of thought.

Chapter Three

Monkeyshines

IF YOU HAPPENED to own a monkey in the spring of 1925, you had it made. Not many people did own monkeys in rural Tennessee, but a few had them as pets or as attractions in small-time zoos. And it seemed that all of a sudden, everyone was obsessed with monkeys. If you had a monkey to sell, you could name your own price.

The most controversial, and for many people the most infuriating, part of Darwin's theory was the concept that humans were descended from apes. Many who accepted the fact that species could change over time were outraged by Darwin's claim that humans and

"Joe Mendi" was the name given to a trained chimpanzee by his handlers, Roland Roberts and Gertrude Bauman. They brought the famous chimp to Dayton to cash in on the monkey craze.

monkeys had common ancestors.

Did Darwin really say we descended from monkeys? In 1871, Charles Darwin published an even more shocking book than *On the Origin of Species*. In *The Descent of Man*, Darwin wrote, "Man is descended from a hairy, tailed quadruped, probably arboreal in its habits, and

A Venerable Orang-outang

A CONTRIBUTION TO UNNATURAL HISTORY

This image appeared in 1871 in the *Hornet*, a British satirical magazine, after the publication of *The Descent of Man*. Charles Darwin was often mocked and criticized for his theory that humans had evolved from apes. The elderly scientist had a good sense of humor, however, and enjoyed collecting the cartoons. "I keep all those things," he told a friend. "Have you seen me in the *Hornet*?"

an inhabitant of the Old World." Humans, monkeys, orangutans, baboons, gorillas: All came from the same original ancestor, and evolved into distinct species over vast eons of time. Chimpanzees are our nearest relatives, but humans and chimps became separate species millions of years ago.

For many people, the thought that humans were not superior to all "lower creatures" was appalling. And to be grouped with ugly, smelly, funny-looking monkeys was a repulsive thought. "Your old man's a monkey!" became the ultimate playground insult. But for a lot of people, the whole monkey business went much deeper than a joke.

The idea that people were descended from apes provoked powerful emotions of fury and terror. Darwin's theory implied that humans were *not* created in God's image, as the Bible claimed. Did this mean that humans were not especially loved and guided by their divine Creator? For many, this frightening idea undermined

HUNTER'S *CIVIC BIOLOGY*

Although we know that man is separated mentally by a wide gap from all other animals, in our study of physiology we must ask where we are to place man. If we attempt to classify man, we see at once he must be placed with the vertebrate animals because of his possession of a vertebral column. Evidently, too, he is a mammal, because the young are nourished by milk secreted by the mother and because his body has at least a partial covering of hair. Anatomically we find that we must place man with the apelike mammals, because of these numerous points of structural likeness. The group of mammals which includes the monkeys, apes, and man we call the primates.

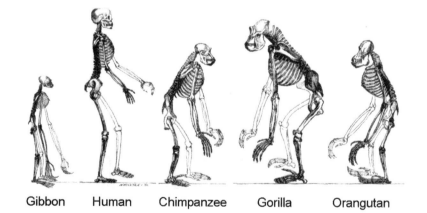

Gibbon   Human   Chimpanzee   Gorilla   Orangutan

everything they believed in. If children were taught that Genesis was just a fable, would they begin to doubt all the miracles described in the Bible? Would they doubt Jesus's virgin birth? Would they even turn away from the very cornerstone of the Christian faith, Christ's resurrection from the dead? To Fundamentalists like Bryan, it was clear: "If evolution wins, Christianity goes!"

People were repelled and horrified—yet strangely fascinated—by the glimpse of our ancient past that Darwin had unveiled. As news of the "Scopes affair" spread across the country, zoos reported a huge spike in attendance. Crowds stood in front of monkey cages, joking, laughing—and wondering if they were looking at relatives. A Baltimore reporter named H. L. Mencken referred to the upcoming trial of John Scopes as the "Monkey Trial," and the name stuck. Soon the national press was referring to Dayton as "Monkeytown"—for good reason.

"'Monkey' has become the most important word in Dayton's vocabulary," wrote one reporter. Dayton businessmen weren't much interested in debating theology versus biology—but they scented a golden opportunity for advertising.

Billboards sprang up featuring monkeys drinking soda or holding bottles of cure-all medicine. A delivery truck had a sign: MONKEYVILLE EXPRESS. The butcher shop's sign announced WE HANDLE ALL KINDS OF MEAT—EXCEPT MONKEY!

A disapproving group of citizens known as the

Dayton Progressive League passed a resolution asking the town merchants to maintain a proper dignity, but it didn't have much effect. Seemed like every shop front had a live monkey in the window. Stretching over Doc Robinson's now-famous drugstore was a huge banner: WHERE IT ALL STARTED. Inside the crowded store, you could buy treats like "Monkey Fizz" and "Simian Sundaes." (You couldn't get a copy of Hunter's *Civic Biology*,

Robinson's Drug Store soon became a jam-packed tourist attraction. Visitors mobbed the ice cream counter during the torrid weather of the trial.

though—the controversial textbooks were sold out.)

And things weren't going to quiet down anytime soon. The pace of the usually slow-grinding legal system was kicking into high gear. The next step in the process was to have a grand jury decide whether the evidence showed that John Scopes should be put on trial. Ordinarily, the grand jury wasn't scheduled to meet until fall, but such was the fever of national interest that a special session was called for May 25.

According to the Butler Act, teaching evolution was a minor crime known as a misdemeanor. Common misdemeanors included offenses like urinating in public, or being drunk and disorderly. A serious crime, like murder or rape, was called a felony, and carried more severe punishments. Usually, people who committed misdemeanors weren't put on trial—they only had to appear before a judge and pay a fine. But the publicity surrounding the Scopes trial was so immense, the authorities decided a grand jury session was warranted, to formally accuse the teacher of breaking the law.

John Scopes had admitted to committing the crime. But the funny thing was that he couldn't remember having said the word "evolution" in the classroom. Even years afterward, John could never recall if he really had taught evolution on that day or not! He had certainly reviewed sections of the textbook while prepping the students for an exam, but no one could remember for sure if he had covered the paragraphs on evolution.

But John was determined to fight this law, and to do that he had to be indicted. With the help of his lawyer, John Neal, he chose seven students as witnesses, including Howard Morgan, Bud Shelton, and five other boys. Finding that none of them could remember much about the lesson, he drilled them in the basics of Darwinism. Professor Scopes was a good teacher, and soon the boys could recite paragraphs of evolutionary theory by heart.

The boys were very reluctant to testify at the grand jury hearing. They all liked Mr. Scopes. Rhea Central High School had frequent assembly programs on citizenship, but John had found the speeches pompous and boring, so during the assemblies he would often hold "wide-open bull sessions" in his classroom in the school basement. He and some of the boys would hang out, smoking illicit cigarettes and kicking around ideas.

"They discussed whatever came to mind," John remembered, "and how they talked! Science, ethics, politics, or any peculiar wrinkle of life would be brought to the forum, until the boys, exploring their intellectual horizons as they did in no organized class, had exhausted their views." He encouraged them to speak their minds and form their own opinions.

Scopes and Neal both realized that the students' testimony might not be literally true, but there was no other way to get the case into the courts. The boys did as their teacher asked, and testified before the grand jury that Mr. Scopes had taught evolution.

After the boys had been heard, Judge John Raulston read aloud the controversial passage from Hunter's *Civic Biology*. He also read the entire first chapter of Genesis from the Bible, which describes God's creation of the world and all living creatures, including humans.

Judge Raulston was a popular town resident who

Genesis

CHAPTER 1

In the beginning God created the heaven and the earth. And the earth was without form, and void; and darkness was upon the face of the deep. And the Spirit of God moved upon the face of the waters. And God said, Let there be light: and there was light. And God saw the light, that it was good: and God divided the light from the darkness. And God called the light Day, and the darkness he called Night. And the evening and the morning were the first day.

And God said, Let there be a firmament in the midst of the waters, and let it divide the waters from the waters. And God made the firmament, and divided the waters which were under the firmament from the waters which were above the firmament: and it was so.

And God called the firmament Heaven. And the evening and the morning were the second day.

And God said, Let the waters under the heaven be gathered together unto one place, and let the dry land appear: and it was so. And God called the dry land Earth; and the gathering together of the waters he called Seas: and God saw that it was good. And God said, Let the earth bring forth grass, the herb yielding seed, and the fruit tree yielding fruit after his kind, whose seed is in itself, upon the earth: and it was so . . . And the evening and the morning were the third day.

And God said, Let there be lights in the firmament of the heaven to divide the day from the night; and let them be for signs, and for seasons, and for days, and years . . . And God made two great lights; the greater light to rule the day, and the lesser light to rule the night: he made the stars also . . . And the evening and the morning were the fourth day.

And God said, Let the waters bring forth abundantly the moving creature that hath life, and fowl that may fly above the earth . . . And the evening and the morning were the fifth day.

And God said, Let the earth bring forth the living creature after his kind, cattle, and creeping thing, and beast of the earth after his kind . . . And God said, Let us make man in our image, after our likeness: and let them have dominion over the fish of the sea, and over the fowl of the air, and over the cattle, and over all the earth, and over every creeping thing that creepeth upon the earth. So God created man in his own image, in the image of God created he him; male and female created he them. And God blessed them, and God said unto them, Be fruitful, and multiply, and replenish the earth, and subdue it: and have dominion over the fish of the sea, and over the fowl of the air, and over every living thing that moveth upon the earth . . . And God saw every thing that he had made, and, behold, it was very good. And the evening and the morning were the sixth day.

had been elected judge of the Eighteenth Circuit Court of Tennessee, the legal district that included Dayton. He was also a preacher at the Methodist church, and frequently spoke at church services. It's customary for judges to maintain the appearance of being impartial toward cases they preside over, but from the start Judge Raulston made no secret of his deep faith in the Bible.

To no one's surprise, John Scopes was indicted. The trial date was set for July 10. If he was found guilty, the penalty wasn't too dreadful: a fine of not less than a hundred dollars, but not more than five hundred dollars.

After the grand jury session, eager reporters crowded around the boys. One reporter asked Howard Morgan how he liked learning about Darwin's theories. "I lapped it up," Howard assured the reporter. "All about monkeys and things." However, it was apparent that Professor Scopes hadn't convinced all his students of the truth of evolution. Howard told reporters: "I believe in part of evolution, but I don't believe in the monkey business."

The untidy law professor John Neal had so far been Scopes's only legal advisor, but he would soon have lots of company. As the trial date drew closer, more lawyers joined the fray—and each of them had their own agenda.

For Neal, the issue of academic freedom was the most important. He summed up the situation: "The question is not whether evolution is true or untrue, but whether one shall have the freedom to teach or learn." But the staff of the ACLU felt that broader ideas were at stake. Not just university professors and high school teachers were threatened by the Butler Act.

Freedom of speech is guaranteed to all Americans in the Constitution of the United States, and the ACLU wanted to focus on that issue. They assembled a team of experts in constitutional law. Dudley Field Malone was a New York City lawyer, who Scopes called "a model of the well-dressed man." Malone wouldn't tolerate so much as a wrinkle in his trim, fashionable suits. Arthur Garfield Hays was another Manhattan lawyer, and one of the original founders of the ACLU.

The defense team was just beginning to plan strategy when they were interrupted by stunning news. Yet another lawyer wanted to get in on the act. A Chicago criminal attorney named Clarence Darrow announced publicly that he was volunteering his services for the defense.

Darrow was familiar to drama-loving newspaper readers. He had been the star of a series of sensational trials, defending child murderers, bombers, and arsonists—with astounding success. He often worked for free, representing people on the fringes of society, such as Black workers, union organizers, and poor women, and he reveled in cases that were controversial or unpopular. Clarence Darrow would later be known as "the attorney for the damned."

He was often accused of being an atheist: someone

who denies the existence of any god. In private, Darrow had sometimes admitted to friends that this was true. Publicly, however, he called himself an agnostic: someone who is unsure

if God exists. Atheist or not, Darrow believed fervently that religion had no place in government—or in the classrooms of public schools. He wanted to focus on the crucial issue of the separation of church and state.

The ACLU team urged Scopes to turn Darrow down. They feared that Darrow's rejection of religion and his abrasive style would infuriate people, and that his fame would divert attention from the issue of constitutional

Clarence Darrow was the most famous lawyer of his day, a rock-star celebrity. He loved the challenge of a case that seemed impossible to win.

rights. But John Scopes knew he needed a strong voice to oppose William Jennings Bryan's fiery speech-making.

John Scopes had majored in law—and he had also coached football. He knew the days ahead would be a "down-in-the-mud fight." A strong offense was crucial. He needed a fighter, not dignified, well-dressed "suits" from the big city. Scopes defied the ACLU and made the call. He wanted Darrow, and that was that.

Now the battle lines were drawn, and the reporters really began to pour in. As spring went on and the weather grew hotter and more humid, trainloads of journalists arrived in Dayton. They came from small towns in Tennessee and Kentucky, and from America's biggest cities: New York, Chicago, St. Louis. The quiet little town was becoming a congested, noisy place. Hotels were charging record-breaking prices: as much as eight dollars a night for a bed! Many Dayton residents started making good money renting rooms. Most of the reporters bunked in Bailey's Hardware, which was turned into a sort of dormitory/news center, with a single outdoor latrine. The hardware store echoed to the sound of typewriters clattering, as reporters documented the preparations for what they were calling "the Trial of the Century."

Telegraph operators from Western Union set up shop in a back room of the grocery store. They began tapping out hundreds of thousands of words, letter by letter in Morse code, to press services around the world. Articles on the "Monkey Trial" were featured in newspapers in England, Italy, Germany, Russia, China, Japan. As July began, the circus was in full swing.

USUALLY THE EXPRESS train from the nearby city of Chattanooga went rushing right through small towns like Dayton. But on July 7, three days before the start of the trial, the train made a special stop. Practically the entire town turned out to welcome William Jennings Bryan as he got off the train, accompanied by his adoring wife, Mary. Bryan was sixty-five, a big, portly man with a fringe of hair around his bald head. Dressed in a dark suit with natty bow tie, he wore a white pith helmet for protection from the fierce southern sun.

Many of Dayton's citizens weren't particularly interested in evolution, but they were thrilled by the visit of such an A-list celebrity. The school superintendent made a speech hailing the famous visitor as the nation's greatest man. That night, the Progressive Club gave the biggest banquet in Dayton's history in Bryan's honor. To John's astonishment, not only was he invited to the party, but he was given a seat at the head table, right next to the man who would prosecute him.

"I know you!" Bryan exclaimed the instant he set eyes on Scopes. "I think you're one of those high school students who made a disturbance at the commencement address I delivered in Salem several years ago." John was amazed to be recognized after a gap of six years. He stammered that he respected Bryan even though they held different opinions, and Bryan apparently held no grudge. "Good!" he said pleasantly. "We shall get along fine."

In spite of the amiable dinner party, and all the monkeyshines in town, things were beginning to get serious. Scopes put it bluntly: "With the arrival of Bryan, the theme in Dayton had changed fast, from the monkey business to the God business."

John Scopes remembered the craziness for the rest of his life. "There never was anything else like this," he wrote. "It was a carnival from start to finish. Every Bible-shouting psalm-singing pulpit hero in the state poured out of the hills and brought his soapbox with him, and they came from outside the state, too."

In the days before the trial, a brutal heat wave began to grip the town. But not even the hot, humid weather could discourage the people pouring into Dayton.

Fundamentalist supporters arrived from farms and hill country all over the rural South. A *New York Times* reporter described the procession: "They came in small automobiles . . . they came in wagons . . . drawn by big-legged horses and small-legged mules. Some came on foot. All were sober-faced, tight-lipped, expressionless, for they were to witness, it seemed to them, a battle for the Lord." They were eager to see their idol, William Jennings Bryan, who was especially popular—almost worshipped—in the region of the Deep South known as the Bible Belt. Many had grown up listening to Bryan's resonant voice preaching the word of God on the radio.

THE TOWN WAS flooded with out-of-town evangelists: preachers who were on a mission to convert others to their Fundamentalist beliefs. Also, churches of many denominations sent representatives to observe the trial. Most of these were clergymen who were wholeheartedly for the prosecution, but a few were on the side of the defense. One was Reverend W. H. Moses, a Black Baptist pastor. He mingled with the crowds around the courthouse, wearing a formal suit and tie in spite of the dreadful heat. He wrote that he hoped the trial would demonstrate that "Christianity is strengthened by science rather than weakened."

Many people came for the thrill, eager to experience the show of a lifetime. Missionaries stood on soapboxes to shout warnings of hellfire and damnation. Choirs sang hymns on street corners. Big-city reporters were especially fascinated by the wildly dancing worshippers from the backwoods known as Holy Rollers, who would sometimes roll on the ground in religious ecstasy.

The evangelist T. T. Martin, who founded a group called the Anti-Evolution League, did a brisk business selling his book titled *Hell and the High Schools: Christ or Evolution—Which?* This popular work insisted that the study of evolution was "the greatest curse that ever fell upon this earth." He railed against "the teachers, paid by our taxes, who feed our children's minds with the deadly, soul-destroying poison of Evolution," and implored parents to save their children's immortal souls from damnation. Any child who studied evolution risked spending eternity in hell.

John knew that he had triggered all this frantic activity and publicity. More and more reporters descended on Dayton, an estimated two hundred in all, constantly looking for a scoop, a new angle, the next shocking headline.

The trial would be covered not just in print, but on the air. The Rhea County Courthouse was being rigged with a tangled web of wires. The radio station WGN was

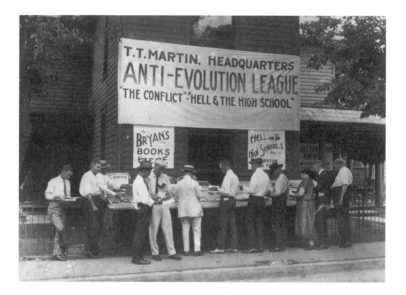

T. T. Martin's anti-evolution books, with titles like God—or Gorilla?, *compared teaching evolution to giving children poisoned candy.*

preparing to broadcast the trial live over the radio.

WGN was a radio network based in Chicago, only a year old. Each day of the Scopes trial, they paid $1,000 (about $15,000 today) to rent telephone lines to carry their broadcasts live across the nation. Radio was such a new technology that it still seemed a bit like science fiction, and local citizens regarded the radio staff with awe. "We're like moon men here," Quin Ryan, the WGN announcer, commented when he arrived in town. "We're the radio guys from outer space!" The mayor of Dayton invited the radio staff to stay at his house during the trial.

It would be the first live broadcast of a trial in history. Judge Raulston gave the WGN engineers

Dayton just couldn't get enough of monkeys.

permission to set up the courtroom as they pleased, and the jury box was moved from its usual place in the center of the room to make space for microphones. A special seat was reserved for Ryan, who would narrate events play-by-play like a sportscaster. Unfortunately, none of the trial broadcasts were recorded, since recording technology were still being developed.

On the eve of the trial, the streets of "Monkeytown" were choked with sightseers. Trained monkeys did tricks for pennies, and people paid to have their photographs taken posing with a chimpanzee dressed in a suit and tie.

John longed to escape from the circus. But it was too late now. The main event was about to begin.

MEDIA IN THE SPOTLIGHT:

RADIO

In the 1920s, radio was a glamorous new technology. Radio broadcasting had been pioneered in the late 1800s, but it required complex equipment and was used by only a few experts. During World War I, the United States government controlled all radio for military use. But as soon as the war ended in 1918, the government made radio licenses available to the public. Hundreds of radio stations took to the airwaves almost overnight.

From the start, radio was a money-making business. Broadcasts were funded by advertising dollars, and most radio stations were owned by local businesses or big companies. Audiences

listened to programs that touted the names of products, like "The Champion Spark Plug Hour" or "General Motors Concerts."

The technology for recording sound was still being developed, so all radio broadcasts were live. The first live sporting event, a boxing match, was broadcast in 1921. Radio caught on rapidly, and by 1925 more than five million homes in America had radios.

Chapter Four

"Do You Know Anything About Evolution?"

READ YOUR BIBLE.

The giant words were painted on a banner four feet high, draped on the redbrick wall of the courthouse where the "Monkey Trial" was about to start. No one knew who had placed the sign, but it loomed over the crowd assembling for the trial's first day.

The Rhea County Courthouse was a large, dignified building with an imposing arched doorway and a high clock tower. Usually, it was a quiet place where legal business was transacted. But on the morning of July 10, the road leading to the courthouse was like a carnival midway. The street was blocked off to car traffic and lined with stalls where vendors hawked watermelon, popcorn, fried chicken, and Bibles. Some local musicians played lively tunes, while others played hymns. Evangelists preached sermons about the dangers of "evil-ution." Many enterprising youngsters had set up lemonade stands and were busily serving thirsty customers, as the temperature had already risen into the nineties.

The Rhea County Courthouse was a peaceful place—until the morning of July 10, 1925.

Even the extra bathrooms set up behind the courthouse were used to spread the word.

AS SOON AS the courthouse doors opened, people hurried into the building and trampled up the stairs. The large courtroom on the second floor had been well prepared for the event, with the addition of five hundred extra chairs, a movie camera platform, and a fresh coat of paint. New public toilets had been added downstairs, draped with another READ YOUR BIBLE banner.

The crowd poured into the room, vying for chairs. About a hundred of the throng were reporters, who headed straight for their reserved seats up front. Also in the crowd were telegraph operators, ready to tap out the lawyers' words in Morse code. These dot-dash-dot signals could travel over hundreds of miles of wires and go directly to newspaper offices so that write-ups of the events could be printed in the paper, often on the same day.

The rest of the crowd was a mix of all sorts of people: ministers and churchmen, farmers, housewives, shopkeepers, and businessmen. Many of John Scopes's high school students were there, along with their families, including Howard Morgan, Bud Shelton, and others who were going to be called as witnesses. The courtroom was not racially segregated, and several Black spectators were in the crowd.

Spectators who couldn't fit in the courtroom had to settle for benches outside, but it was much cooler under the shady maples on the courthouse lawn.

Soon every seat was filled, and it was standing room only. More than a thousand people managed to squeeze themselves inside, while hundreds more thronged the courthouse lawn, where benches and loudspeakers had been set up so that those who couldn't fit indoors could listen to the excitement.

With all the people crammed together in the courtroom, the heat rose steadily—and so did the smell of sweating bodies. The crowd waited, cooling themselves with round palm-leaf fans. Hundreds of these lightweight fans had been distributed as advertising by a local dentist, printed with an ominous question: *Do your gums bleed?*

A stir of excitement rippled through the crowd, and heads turned to face the courtroom doors. The stars of the show were arriving.

The defense team began to squeeze their way through the crowd. Clarence Darrow shambled along, looking casual and relaxed, his coat unbuttoned and sparse gray hair falling over his forehead. The sixty-eight-year-old Darrow seemed like a kindly grandfather, nodding pleasantly to everyone. "His huge head, leathery lined face, square jaw, his twisted mouth of the skeptic, are softened by the quizzical twinkle of his deep-set eyes," wrote a reporter. He was accompanied by the other lawyers: Dudley Field Malone, neatly buttoned up in a New York City suit; John Neal, unkempt as always; and the ACLU attorney Arthur Garfield Hays. Last came John Scopes himself, in a white shirt and bow tie. He had to push his way through the throng, tensely aware of the gaze of a thousand people trained on his face.

The crowd broke into cheers as William Jennings Bryan entered. Quin Ryan, the WGN commentator, narrated the entrance in a hushed, dramatic tone: "Here comes William Jennings Bryan. He enters now. His bald pate like a sunrise over Key West." Bryan was

John Scopes at the center of the storm.

an imposing figure, tall and stout. Seven other lawyers trailed him, including Tom Stewart, the local district attorney, and Sue Hicks, the Dayton lawyer who was a friend of Scopes's and had suggested his name in Doc Robinson's drugstore.

Bryan walked majestically over to greet the defense team. Photographers and newsreel cameramen stood on chairs to record the scene as Bryan and Darrow shook hands. The two famous men knew each other

Darrow and Bryan both knew that a fierce, bitter struggle lay ahead, and that only one of them could win.

well. Once, they had been on the same side.

For decades, both men had defended the rights of the "common man": factory workers toiling for little pay in dangerous conditions, child laborers, bankrupt farmers. When Bryan made his first run for president in 1896, Clarence Darrow had been one of his most ardent supporters. Darrow had worked hard for Bryan's campaign, in which he was a strong contender, winning 47 percent of the popular vote.

But those exciting days were long past. Bryan was now focusing all his energy and star power on this one issue of evolution in the classroom, and he and Darrow were at opposite poles. Darrow passionately opposed what he called the ignorance and bigotry of denying science and forcing religion into public classrooms. With equal passion, Bryan opposed evolution being taught in schools, sowing doubt and disbelief in the minds of children. They had debated the issue before, in the newspapers.

Two years before the Scopes trial, William Jennings Bryan was writing dozens of anti-evolution articles and letters to newspaper editors. One, addressed to Darrow's hometown paper, the *Chicago Tribune*, stated Bryan's position on the teaching of Darwinism—he did not insist that it be totally banned from the classroom, only that it not be taught "as true."

WILLIAM JENNINGS BRYAN'S LETTER TO THE EDITOR

Chicago Tribune
June 20, 1923

To the Editor:

You . . . misrepresent my attitude on the teaching of Darwinism. My views are set forth in a resolution unanimously adopted by the Legislature of Florida, expressing it as the sense of the Legislature "that it is improper and subversive of the best interest of the people of this state for any professor, teacher or instructor in the public schools or colleges of this state, supported in whole or in part by public taxation, to teach or permit to be taught atheism or agnosticism or to teach as true Darwinism, or any other hypothesis that links man in blood relationship to any other form of life." . . .

We are, Mr. Editor, engaged in a controversy which church members, whether conservative or radical, regard as a very serious one—a contest upon the result of which depends the power of the Christian church to prosecute its work . . .

Very truly yours,

William Jennings Bryan

Clarence Darrow responded in the *Tribune* with a letter to the editor of his own, posing a list of questions on the miraculous events described in the Bible and challenging Bryan to answer. Bryan refused to comment.

CLARENCE DARROW'S LETTER TO THE EDITOR

Chicago Tribune
July 4, 1923

To the Editor:

A few questions to Mr. Bryan and the Fundamentalists, if fairly answered, might serve the interests of reaching the truth—all of this assumes that truth is desirable. For this reason I think it would be helpful if Mr. Bryan would answer the following questions:

- Do you believe in the literal interpretation of the whole Bible?

- Was the earth made in six literal days, measured by the revolution of the earth on its axis?

- Did God place man in the Garden of Eden and tell him he could eat of every tree except the tree of knowledge?

- Did the serpent induce Eve to eat from the tree of knowledge?

(cont'd)

- Did God curse the serpent for tempting Eve and decree that thereafter he should go [crawl] on his belly?

- How did he travel before that time?

- Did God tell Eve that thereafter he would multiply the sorrows of all women and that their husbands should rule over them? . . .

Can one not be a Christian without believing in the literal truth of the narrations of the Bible here mentioned? Would you forbid the public schools from teaching anything in conflict with the literal statements referred to? Questions might be extended indefinitely, but a specific answer to these might make it clear what one must believe to be a "Fundamentalist."

Very truly yours,

Clarence Darrow

Clarence Darrow

Judge Raulston was already at the front of the courtroom, mingling with friends and reporters. He was a pleasant-faced, plump man wearing a simple lightweight suit. (Tennessee judges didn't usually wear formal black robes.) He cheerfully posed with Bryan, Darrow, and the other lawyers for a photo shoot. Then the judge took his seat and banged the gavel for quiet. The first order of business, as always in Tennessee courts, was to open the proceedings with a long and heartfelt prayer.

Reverend Cartwright, a local Fundamentalist minister, prayed at length that "the Holy Spirit may be with the jury and with the accused and with the attorneys" so that they would be "loyal to God." Darrow and the other defense lawyers stared out the window with expressionless faces, but the audience listened with enthusiasm, punctuating the long prayer with shouts of "Amen!"

There were many legal details to be addressed before the trial could start, and the lawyers droned on through the long, hot morning and, after a short lunch break, into the afternoon. Then, at last, it was finally time to get down to business in the case of *The State of Tennessee v. John Thomas Scopes*. The next question was, who would decide if John was guilty or innocent?

At the beginning of a trial, twelve jurors are chosen during a process called *voir dire*. Prospective jurors are randomly selected from the local citizens, and questioned by both the defense and the prosecution to see if they can be fair and impartial. Almost every man in Dayton was hoping to be chosen as a juror, in order to get a ringside seat at this exciting show.

There was no question that the jury would be all male—and all white. Women were not allowed to serve on juries in the state of Tennessee until 1951. Black men had the legal right to serve as jurors, but in the 1920s racial prejudices were so strong that it was almost un-

Clarence Darrow's suspenders were almost as famous as he was, and he had worn them at many notorious trials.

heard of for a Black man to be considered as a juror, especially in a southern state like Tennessee.

Usually, Clarence Darrow spent weeks questioning hundreds of possible jurors, to discover anyone who might be prejudiced against his client. But in this case, Darrow knew that all the prospective jurors were local citizens who had been hotly debating the case for weeks. He settled for trying to weed out anyone who was strongly opposed to the teaching of evolution. John, sitting silently behind a long table with the other defense lawyers, listened as Darrow questioned each man.

The airless courtroom was so hot that the judge had given permission for coats to be removed, and Darrow was in shirtsleeves and wearing his favorite purple suspenders. For Darrow, the suspenders did more than just hold his pants up—the old-fashioned galluses were his trademark, and one of his favorite props. He hooked his thumbs in them, snapped them loudly to get a laugh, and used them to lure juries into thinking him a folksy, nonthreatening fellow.

As each would-be juror was called to the front, Darrow would approach with thumbs hooked in his colorful suspenders. He asked essentially the same questions of each man: "Do you know anything about evolution?" was the first. He continued with "Did you ever have any opinion . . . on whether the Bible was against evolution or not?" When he asked a local farmer if he had ever read anything about evolution, the man responded, "I can't read!"

"Is that due to your eyes?" Darrow inquired.

"No, I am uneducated," the man replied with simple dignity. Darrow accepted him as a juror.

When one potential juror admitted to being a minister, Darrow asked if he had ever preached about evolution. "I preached against it, of course!" the minister snapped. The audience applauded loudly, but Darrow refused him a place on the jury.

Eventually, twelve men were selected. Instead of weeks, the jury selection process took only two hours. Darrow did his best, but there were few evolution fans in the town of Dayton. "It was obvious," H. L. Mencken wrote, "that the jury would be unanimously hot for Genesis. The most that Mr. Darrow could hope for was to

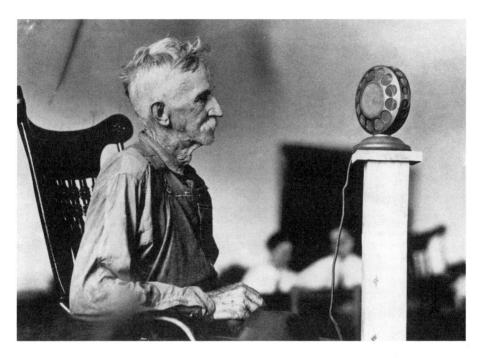

Of the twelve jurors chosen, nine were farmers.

Judge Raulston, right, and the twelve jurymen. The judge and eleven of the jurors were regular churchgoers.

sneak in a few men bold enough to declare publicly that they would have to hear the evidence against Scopes before condemning him."

H. L. Mencken was a well-known journalist for the *Baltimore Sun*. He was in Dayton not as a reporter but to write editorials that were his own opinions. And he had some *very* strong opinions. He was appalled by what he called "this Tennessee buffoonery." He sneered at the ignorance of the rural spectators, calling them hicks and yokels. In a scathing essay titled "*Homo Neanderthalensis,*" he claimed that the Fundamentalists in "these forlorn backwaters" seeking to ban the teaching of evolution were "vermin," and railed, "They are ignorant, they are dishonest, they are cowardly, they are ignoble. They know little if anything that is worth knowing, and there is not the slightest sign of a natural desire among them to increase their knowledge."

Mencken's articles amused his northern big-city readers, but infuriated rural southerners. His insults were one of the causes of the bitter divide between urban people and country folk that was beginning to infect the nation and would only deepen with time.

As soon as jury selection was over, it was time to adjourn for the weekend. The judge banged the gavel, and the crowd gladly abandoned the stifling courtroom. Everyone streamed out into the fresh air, which was perfumed with the delicious scent of four whole steers roasting in huge barbecue pits. The lemonade stands

HOMO NEANDERTHALENSIS

Editorial by H. L. Mencken • *Baltimore Evening Sun,* June 29, 1925

Such obscenities as the forthcoming trial of the Tennessee evolutionist, if they serve no other purpose, at least call attention dramatically to the fact that enlightenment, among mankind, is very narrowly dispersed. It is common to assume that human progress affects everyone—that even the dullest man, in these bright days, knows more than any man of, say, the Eighteenth Century, and is far more civilized. This assumption is quite erroneous . . .

Such immortal vermin, true enough, get their share of the fruits of human progress, and so they may be said, in a way, to have their part in it. The most ignorant man, when he is ill, may enjoy whatever boons and usufructs modern medicine may offer . . . The literature of the world is at his disposal in public libraries. He may look at works of art. He may hear good music. He has at hand a thousand devices for making life less wearisome and more tolerable: the telephone, railroads, bichloride tablets, newspapers, sewers, correspondence schools, delicatessens. But he had no more to do with bringing these things into the world than the horned cattle in the fields, and he does no more to increase them today than the birds of the air.

On the contrary, he is generally against them, and sometimes with immense violence.

Every step in human progress, from the first feeble stirrings in the abyss of time, has been opposed by the great majority of men. Every valuable thing that has been added to the store of man's possessions has been derided by them when it was new, and destroyed by them when they had the power. They have fought every new truth ever heard of, and they have killed every truth-seeker who got into their hands.

were mobbed. It was Friday night, and time to party.

The hordes of reporters waited impatiently for the weekend to be over, anxious for new material for their readers. John enjoyed a break from the tension, and went to a Saturday-night dance at a local hotel. Bryan made a speech on the courthouse lawn, which was attended by thousands of the faithful. On Sunday he preached a sermon at a Dayton church, with Judge Raulston and his family seated in a front pew. Meanwhile, Darrow and the other defense lawyers huddled in their boardinghouse, planning strategy.

They realized that this was most likely an unwinnable case. The judge was making no secret of where his sympathies lay. The jury certainly wasn't on their side. And their defendant had admitted his guilt. Eyewitnesses were prepared to swear to it. Clearly, John Scopes had broken the law.

But the defense team came up with a strategy that—they hoped—could change all that. What if the Butler Act was a law that never should have existed? The defense was planning to ask a simple question that could derail the whole proceeding—was this law legal? Instead of John Scopes, the law itself would be on trial.

Chapter Five

"The Fires That Have Been Lighted in America"

Be it enacted by the General Assembly of Tennessee, that it shall be unlawful for any teacher . . . in the state to teach any theory that denies the story that the earth is in the center of the universe as taught in the Bible, and to teach instead that the earth and planets move around the sun.

Be it further enacted that any teacher found guilty of a violation of this act shall be guilty of a felony, and upon conviction shall be put to death.

ARTHUR GARFIELD HAYS, the ACLU's constitutional law expert, wasn't serious when he proposed this law. It was part of the defense's strategy to convince the court that the Butler Act was a ridiculous law that should never have been passed.

When court convened bright and early Monday morning, the temperature was as torrid as ever—Tennessee was still in the heat wave's grip, with the thermometer edging up to one hundred degrees every day. But the courtroom was filled to overflowing. Most people were uncomfortably sandwiched in by their sweating neighbors, but the twelve jurymen enjoyed roomy seats in the jury box and were cooled by an electric fan. Everyone settled in for a long day, expecting the trial to continue on the usual lines: prosecution, defense, verdict. But as soon as the judge banged the gavel, everything went off the rails.

The usual trial process came to an abrupt halt when defense attorney John Neal, unshaven and untidy as ever, proposed a motion that John Scopes's indictment should be thrown out, because the Butler Act was a law that never should have been made. It was, he argued, in direct violation of the Constitution of the United States.

The U.S. Constitution was ratified in 1788, and outlines the principles and structure of the United States government. No law, even a state law, is valid if it conflicts with the Constitution.

Judge Raulston realized that now the spotlight was suddenly turned on him. He had been a judge for years, but had usually presided over cases involving traffic violations, or the making of illegal whiskey. Determining whether a law was constitutional was a weighty decision that would make headlines across the nation.

His first act was to excuse the jury—not that they wanted to be excused. The jurymen were bitterly disappointed that they couldn't remain in the courtroom, and grumbled loudly as they were ushered out. But it was usual legal practice to have the jury leave whenever a topic was discussed that might prejudice them. So the jury were not allowed to hear any of the long debate that followed. Much to their disgust, they spent the next two days waiting impatiently, hanging about outside the courtroom.

Arthur Garfield Hays continued the argument for the defense: The law was unconstitutional because the Constitution called for the separation of church and state. But the Butler Act made the Bible, a religious document, the basis of what could be taught in a state-run public school.

Also, he went on, the first ten amendments to the U.S. Constitution, known as the Bill of Rights, guarantee certain rights to all Americans. Freedom of speech is one of the most cherished of these. The defense claimed that John Scopes was being denied this right.

Another part of the Constitution, the Fourteenth Amendment, states that no citizen can be deprived of their liberty without due process of law. That meant, Hays argued, that the Tennessee legislature couldn't make up an absurd law and then imprison someone for disobeying it. To show how unreasonable the Butler Act was, Hays mockingly suggested a law requiring teachers—on pain of death!—to teach that the sun orbits the earth.

The Constitution of the United States

AMENDMENT 1: CONGRESS SHALL MAKE NO LAW RESPECTING AN ESTABLISHMENT OF RELIGION, OR PROHIBITING THE FREE EXERCISE THEREOF; OR ABRIDGING THE FREEDOM OF SPEECH, OR OF THE PRESS; OR THE RIGHT OF THE PEOPLE PEACEABLY TO ASSEMBLE, AND TO PETITION THE GOVERNMENT FOR A REDRESS OF GRIEVANCES.

AMENDMENT 14: NO STATE SHALL MAKE OR ENFORCE ANY LAW WHICH SHALL ABRIDGE THE PRIVILEGES OR IMMUNITIES OF CITIZENS OF THE UNITED STATES; NOR SHALL ANY STATE DEPRIVE ANY PERSON OF LIFE, LIBERTY, OR PROPERTY, WITHOUT DUE PROCESS OF LAW.

Then it was the prosecution's turn to respond. All eyes turned to William Jennings Bryan. But the famous orator sat silent, his sleeves rolled up and collar open, waving his palm-leaf fan.

Bryan wanted to have the last word. He had spent weeks crafting a long and eloquent closing statement, and perhaps he didn't want to use up his ammunition before the trial had really begun. The district attorney, Tom Stewart, presented the prosecution's case.

Stewart was a young man, but he was an experienced,

capable prosecutor, with a stern expression and piercing eyes. He claimed that freedom of speech was not at stake. John Scopes could say whatever he wanted, on his own time. "Mr. Scopes might have taken his stand on the street corners and expounded [evolution] until he

Bryan seemed to feel the effects of the heat in the stifling courtroom.

became hoarse," Stewart said firmly, "but he cannot go into the public schools . . . and teach his theory."

In his unemotional, businesslike statement, Stewart also argued that the First Amendment specifically stated that it only applied to laws made by the United States Congress—laws that affected the entire nation. He pointed out that the state of Tennessee had its own constitution, and the right to make its own laws. Tom Stewart argued that it was up to the voters of Tennessee to decide if they wanted Darwin in their classrooms. "If the state has a right in the exercise of its police power to say you cannot teach Wentworth's arithmetic or Fry's geography [two other popular textbooks], it has the same right to say you cannot teach any theory that denies the divine creation of man," he said. "The legislature is the judge of what shall be taught in the public schools." If teachers could teach whatever they pleased, paying no attention to the wishes of their employers, chaos would result.

The defense had one last chance to respond. And now came the moment that many had been waiting for. A murmur of excitement ran through the courtroom as Clarence Darrow rose. He had been called the most famous criminal lawyer in America. Now the spectators would see if Darrow deserved his reputation as a brilliant defender of hopeless causes. John Scopes listened as Darrow laid out his case, in a speech John remembered for the rest of his life.

Darrow began in a quiet, friendly voice, thanking the judge and the people of Dayton for their courtesy and hospitality. But he soon got to the point. "Here we find today as brazen and bold an attempt to destroy learning as was ever made in the Middle Ages. The only difference is we have not provided that they [teachers] shall be burned at the stake."

Darrow was not himself a religious man, but he could respect those who sincerely believed in the Bible. "I know there are millions of people in the world who derive consolation in their times of trouble and solace in times of distress from the Bible," he assured the court. "But the Bible is a book primarily of religion and morals. It is not a book of science. Never was, and was never meant to be."

Darrow was famous for his fiery, emotional speeches that often lasted for hours.

Darrow had addressed dozens of juries in his long career, but the jury box was empty now—he only had to convince one man, Judge Raulston. Darrow's voice rose, his head thrust forward, his right arm making such forceful gestures that it ripped his shirt at the elbow. "I will tell you what is going to happen," he warned. "Your Honor knows the fires that have been lighted in America to kindle religious bigotry and hate."

Telegraph operators struggled to keep up as they tapped out every word. "While he was talking there was absolute silence in the room except for the clicking of telegraph keys," a reporter from the *New York Times* wrote. "His words fell with crushing force."

H. L. Mencken was in the audience, and he never forgot Darrow's speech. "You have but a dim notion of it who have only read it," he remembered. "It was not designed for reading but for hearing . . . It rose like a wind and ended like a flourish of bugles." The audience sat fanning themselves in silence, while Judge Raulston fidgeted uneasily in his seat.

Darrow ended with a passionate conclusion: "Ignorance and fanaticism is ever busy and needs feeding. Always it is feeding and gloating for more. Today it is the public school teachers, tomorrow the private. The next day . . . the magazines, the books, the newspapers. After a while, Your Honor, it is the setting of man against man and creed against creed until with flying banners and beating drums we are marching backward to the glorious ages of the sixteenth century when bigots . . . burn[ed] the men who dared to bring any intelligence and enlightenment and culture to the human mind."

At the end of the speech, John and the members of the defense team congratulated Darrow heartily. But the spectators were not impressed. There were only a few scattered hand-claps, drowned by low mutters and threats to have Darrow thrown out of the courtroom. Some people hissed to show their disapproval.

The long, hot day was drawing to a close. As soon as Darrow had finished speaking, Judge Raulston immediately adjourned the court, with the issue still undecided. He gave no hint of how he would rule on the defense's motion to dismiss the charges.

Everyone headed outdoors, where the air was only slightly cooler than in the courtroom. Darrow, his throat dry and hoarse from the two-hour speech, joined the throng of people who headed to Doc Robinson's drugstore for ice cream.

That evening, not long after Darrow finished speaking, clouds began to gather overhead. Rising winds and grumbles of distant thunder soon rose to a huge storm. Thunderclaps and flashes of lightning raging over Dayton caused some people to wonder if perhaps the Almighty was expressing his displeasure over the day's events.

It took Judge Raulston a long time to think over the complex issues that both sides had raised. It wasn't until Wednesday morning that the judge announced he was ready.

The thunderstorm had failed to break the heat wave, and the weather was hotter than ever. The crowd in the packed room waited impatiently, swatting flies that came in through the open windows. Judge Raulston sat behind the bench, with a policeman standing alongside, fanning him. In his high-pitched, nasal voice, the judge read aloud a nineteen-page document announcing his ruling: The law was valid. The trial would go on.

Darrow and the other defense lawyers weren't surprised by the result—they knew it had been a long shot. They got ready to move on to the next stage of the proceedings. John wasn't shocked either, but he was bitterly disappointed. He had hoped to walk out of the courtroom a free man, with the Butler Act defeated and all the publicity and frenzy behind him. Now he knew the trial would drag on for many weary days.

After a break for lunch, the irritated jurymen were finally allowed back into the courtroom. The prosecutors were about to present their case. The defense lawyers were lined up at their table, already planning their next move. Everything was ready to proceed—except for one thing.

The defendant was missing. John Scopes was nowhere to be seen.

Chapter Six

"Did He Tell You Anything That Was Wicked?"

JOHN SCOPES PLUNGED into the crystal-clear pond and then surfaced, drops of water running from his sandy hair and down his sun-freckled face. He and two friends had decided to spend the lunchtime recess taking a quick dip in a nearby swimming hole. But just as his students sometimes did, John lost track of time. The minutes went by, and the time came for court to reconvene, but still the three truants soaked in the cool water. The teacher was playing hooky.

Writing about the events of that hot summer forty years later, John still remembered vividly how refreshing the water felt after hours in the stifling courtroom.

"On that summer day it could have been at the end of the world, for we temporarily forgot the trial and everything," he admitted.

Finally, the three young men came back to reality and dragged themselves out of the pond. They hastily returned to court with wet hair and damp clothes. John had a hard time squeezing through the dense crowd to his place at the defense table. Hays, the ACLU lawyer, glared at him. "Where in the hell have you been?" he demanded.

But oddly, the proceedings had resumed anyway, the judge and the prosecutors apparently not noticing the absence of the defendant in the crowded room. Increasingly, John realized he was becoming, as he put it, "a ringside observer at [his] own trial."

He was having bitter second thoughts about the trial, calling it "this fine mess I've gotten myself into." When the idea of standing as a test case was proposed to him, he had envisioned a solemn, businesslike, and brief trial. He had always known that he was very likely to be found guilty. In fact, the ACLU lawyers were hoping he would be.

A guilty verdict would mean that the defense could formally appeal the case to a higher court. This would give them a chance to make their argument about the law being unconstitutional all over again, to the Supreme Court of the State of Tennessee. If those judges still found that Scopes was guilty, the case would go to the highest court in the nation, the United States Supreme Court. The ACLU staff hoped to create a nationwide law protecting the teaching of science.

John knew that appeals could drag on for years, but as the defendant he would not have to be present—lawyers would argue the case before a series of judges. He had expected to be done with the matter in a few days. In fact, he had planned a very different summer, playing tennis and relaxing at dances and ice cream socials, and he had received an offer to work part-time as a car salesman, selling Model-T Fords for a five percent commission. That would have meant quite a bit of money. More than once, John Scopes wished that he could just walk away from it all.

A few things, though, made him soldier on. One was the courtesy and friendliness of the legal teams. Even though they fiercely debated each other in court, once outside the courtroom, prosecutors and defense lawyers were on good terms. When a prosecutor named Ben Mackenzie was overcome by the heat, defense attorney Dudley Malone rushed over to fan him. Even Darrow and Bryan were cordial to each other offstage—at one point Bryan gave Darrow a souvenir gift of a wooden monkey. And the two friends who sneaked off with John to the swimming hole were both prosecutors! The three of them had struck up a friendship: John especially liked the modest young man named William Jennings Bryan, Jr., who was helping his famous father with legal duties.

Another reason for John to stick around was Clarence Darrow. More and more, Scopes was coming to admire the cantankerous older man who could be funny, warm, and friendly—and yet fierce and relentless in the defense of his principles.

The other influence on John Scopes was his father. Thomas Scopes insisted that by taking part in this trial, John was serving his country, the same as a soldier in time of war. Thomas sometimes sat beside John at the defense table, and let it be known that he was proud to have a son who stood up for what was right. John couldn't disappoint him.

Thomas Scopes told a reporter, "A father just naturally has to stick by his own flesh and blood, ma'am—no matter what they've done."

One reason that the prosecutors hadn't noticed John's absence was because they were desperately trying to find their own witnesses. The prosecution planned to call two Dayton high school students, who would testify that Mr. Scopes had taught them the forbidden topic. But in the big room filled with spectators milling around the courtroom as they settled in for the afternoon's festivities, it wasn't easy to locate the two boys they needed. Finally, Tom Stewart spotted them, waiting with their parents at the back of the courtroom. The boys were dressed in their best clothes, perspiring in their ties and formal white shirts.

Howard Morgan, a freshman, and Harry Shelton, a senior, had been among the group of students Mr. Scopes had prepared to give testimony. Howard had already appeared before the grand jury. Now he had to do it all over again—but instead of giving evidence before dozens of people, now he would be stared at by more than a thousand curious faces. The big, shiny microphone, labeled with the call letters WGN, stood right next to the witness chair. Perhaps most intimidating were the cameramen hand-cranking their movie cameras for newsreel footage that would be shown in movie theaters from coast to coast.

The audience was eagerly anticipating the start of the prosecution, hoping for an electrifying speech from William Jennings Bryan. But Bryan still sat watching, while Tom Stewart rose. The first witness called was school superintendent Walter White, who had been at

MEDIA IN THE SPOTLIGHT:

NEWSREELS

After each day of the Scopes trial, the people in Dayton were thrilled by an exciting sight: a plane flying overhead. Airplanes were still rare—they had only been invented twenty years earlier. Aircraft hired by the news media took off from a tiny airstrip outside the town, and would fly low to buzz the waving crowd before roaring off into the sky. They were headed for the big cities: New York, Philadelphia, Chicago, carrying movie footage of the trial.

The film would be processed and developed in a few hours. By next afternoon, clips of courtroom highlights would be showing in theaters. A long string of newsreels and cartoons always ran before the main movie, so that customers got a good show for their twenty-five-cent admission.

Newsreels were entertainment as well as news. One newsreel about the trial livened up dull footage of lawyers and town officials by inserting shots of monkeys chattering and cavorting in trees.

There was one big difference from the movies of today—the technology to add sound to the moving images was still experimental, so at this time movies were completely silent. The images were interspersed with written captions that explained the action. Theaters would often hire a piano player to provide dramatic music. Movies were almost as new and exciting as airplanes. For audiences, watching moving images of people they had only read about or heard over the radio really brought the trial to life and helped to make it a sensational event.

the meeting in Doc Robinson's drugstore. He testified that Scopes had admitted teaching evolution.

Then it was Howard Morgan's turn. He had learned his lessons well, and when he gave his explanation of evolution, defense attorney Arthur Hays called out, "Go to the head of the class!"

Tom Stewart probed into the details of Mr. Scopes's lesson. "I ask you further, Howard," he said, "how did he classify man with reference to other animals; what did he say about them?"

"Well," Howard answered, "the book and he both classified man along with cats and dogs, cows, horses, monkeys, lions, horses, and all that." Howard explained that this grouping of animals was called mammals.

Now it was the defense's turn to cross-examine the young witness. Darrow approached in his most grandfatherly style, and gently questioned the boy. "Now, Howard," Darrow started off, "what do you mean by classify?"

Howard was obviously a little shaky on the details. "Well, it means classify these animals we mentioned, that men were just the same as them."

"He didn't say a cat was the same as a man?" Darrow inquired.

"No, sir," said Howard. "He said man had a reasoning power."

"There is some doubt about that," Darrow said, going for a laugh. His tactic worked—the audience burst into laughter. Darrow often used humor during cross-examinations, which helped make him more likable to the jury.

Darrow continued, "Well, did he tell you anything else that was wicked?"

"No," Howard answered. "Not that I remember."

"It has not hurt you any, has it?"

"No, sir," Howard agreed, to another ripple of laughter in the room.

"It is for the mother of this boy to say what harm this diabolical business has done him!" one of the prosecutors shouted.

Harry Shelton, a seventeen-year-old senior, was up next. In response to Stewart's and Darrow's brief questions, he repeated much of what Howard had said. At the end of the cross-examination, Darrow asked, "Are you a church member?"

"Yes, sir," Harry said.

"Do you still belong?"

"Yes, sir."

Darrow persisted: "You didn't leave church when he told you all forms of life began with a single cell?"

"No, sir," Harry agreed.

After brief questioning of Doc Robinson (who was on the school board as well as running the drugstore) to confirm that Scopes had used Hunter's *Civic Biology*, the prosecution was through with witnesses. Several more of John's students were in the courtroom prepared to testify, but were not called.

Tom Stewart then strode to the front of the room,

picked up a Bible, and read aloud the first two chapters of Genesis. The audience listened respectfully as the beautiful, ancient words rolled out:

In the beginning God created the heaven and the earth.

And the earth was without form, and void; and darkness was upon the face of the deep. And the Spirit of God moved upon the face of the waters.

And God said, Let there be light: and there was light.

And God saw the light, that it was good: and God divided the light from the darkness.

And God called the light Day, and the darkness he called Night.

And the evening and the morning were the first day . . .

Stewart closed the Bible and offered it as Exhibit 2 for the case against John Scopes. Exhibit 1 was a copy of Hunter's *Civic Biology*. Then the prosecution rested its case.

Tom Stewart didn't choose to debate the larger issues of science versus religion. He kept the case clear and simple, and felt he had proven beyond a shadow of a doubt that John Scopes had broken the law. The prosecutors' entire case didn't take long—less than two hours. And still William Jennings Bryan had barely spoken a word before the court.

Chapter Seven

"Will You State What Evolution Is?"

AFTER THE PROSECUTION was finished, it was only midafternoon, so there was time for the other side to get started. Darrow began the defense by admitting, "Your Honor, every single word that they said against this defendant—everything was true."

But the defense team's new strategy was to prove that the Bible and the theory of evolution did not necessarily contradict each other. Many devout people believed that Genesis wasn't a statement of fact, and felt that the biblical verses were poetry, metaphorically describing a process that had taken millions of years. Believing in evolution did not have to mean God did not exist—

evolution was another of God's marvelous creations. In order to make this concept plain to the jury, the defense had spent a big chunk of the ACLU defense fund arranging for a dozen professors of biology, geology, and zoology to travel to Dayton. The scientists had been waiting for days, staying in an uncomfortable, run-down boardinghouse. Dayton town officials referred to it as "Defense Mansion," but the neighbors had christened it the "Monkey House." The scientists enjoyed themselves, though, and John had spent many evenings with them, fascinated by their lively debates and discussions. These eminent men, experts in their fields, were now seated in the courtroom, waiting to be called. All of the scientists were white and male, as few women, white or Black, or people of color held advanced degrees in

The scientists assembled by the defense came from colleges and universities all across the nation. They bunked together in the "Monkey House," a ramshackle building with little plumbing or furniture.

science in the 1920s, and none of them was on Darrow's list to testify. Colleges in Tennessee, as in most of the South, were strictly segregated, and few Black colleges offered science programs.

"We shall show by the testimony of men, leaders in science and theology," Dudley Malone explained, "that there are millions of people who believe in evolution and in stories of creation as set forth in the Bible, and who find no conflict between the two. The defense maintains that this is a matter of faith and interpretation, which each individual must determine for himself."

The plan was for scientist after scientist to explain to the jury—and the rest of the country—what evolution was all about. Well knowing the value of the tremendous publicity the trial was generating, the defense team planned to teach a national biology lesson.

The first witness was Dr. Maynard Metcalf, a professor of zoology from Johns Hopkins University. The defense had been careful to find scientists who were also religious men, and Metcalf was a member of the Congregational church who taught Sunday school classes. A plump figure with gold spectacles, Metcalf sat in the witness seat to explain his qualifications. Then Darrow asked, "Will you state what evolution is, in regard to the origin of man?"

But before Dr. Metcalf could open his mouth, Tom Stewart leaped to his feet. "We except [object] to that!" he called. He claimed that the law outlawed *any* teaching of evolution, period. Whether Darrow's theories conflicted with the Bible or not didn't matter. Anything the professors had to say would be irrelevant. "The state moves to exclude the testimony of the scientists," Stewart said firmly.

The defense lawyers protested, but it wasn't up to them. A judge has the responsibility of deciding what evidence is admissible in court. So once more the spotlight turned to Judge Raulston.

Dr. Maynard Metcalf, the only scientist to be allowed on the witness stand.

Since discussion over allowing expert testimony might prejudice the jury, Raulston immediately excused them. The outraged jurors could hardly believe their ears, but they were once again escorted out the door, fuming. They had spent less than two hours in the courtroom.

Once the jury was out of the way, Dr. Metcalf was allowed to continue his testimony, so that the judge could hear what kind of information the scientists might present. Prompted by Darrow's questions, the professor gave a clear explanation of Darwin's theories. The judge listened intently, but the audience muttered in disgust. Many got up and left. Immediately afterward, court was adjourned for the day.

Next morning, the judge heard arguments for and against the admission of the scientists' expert testimony.

Emotions were running high, and almost every lawyer on both sides took a crack at it. Speech after speech was made. The defense argued that the jury couldn't decide on a law banning evolution if they had no idea what evolution was in the first place. The prosecution claimed the jury was smart enough to think for themselves without the help of so-called experts. Prosecutor Ben Mackenzie got a good laugh when he joked, "Genesis is a much more reasonable story to me than that God threw a substance into the sea and said, 'in sixty thousand years I'll make something of you.'"

After all the speechifying, it was time for lunch. During the long break, an exciting rumor began to spread. People quickly returned to the stuffy courtroom, eager to get a good seat. Spectators filled the doorways and even the halls. Crowds thronged the lawn under the loudspeakers—all drawn by the rumor that at long last William Jennings Bryan was about to speak.

So many people had wedged themselves inside the courtroom that the floorboards creaked ominously. "The floor on which we are now assembled is burdened with a great weight," the judge nervously cautioned the crowd, "so I suggest to you to be as quiet in the courtroom as you can; have no more emotion than you can avoid; especially have no applause."

A hush fell over the room as William Jennings Bryan rose to his feet. He took a drink of water from the pitcher on the table, and then strode forward. Bryan was supposed to be addressing his arguments directly

Bryan got a lot of laughs from his audience, but not as much applause as he had hoped for.

to the judge, but he turned and faced the crowd as though preaching at a revival meeting. Taking a deep breath, he began to speak. His famous voice, familiar to his many fans from evangelical radio broadcasts, was often compared to church bells. It was said he could be

The Doctrine of Evolution. — We have now learned that animal forms may be arranged so as to begin with very simple one-celled forms and culminate with a group which contains man himself. This arrangement is called the *evolutionary series*. Evolution means change, and these groups are believed by scientists to represent stages in complexity of development of life on the earth. Geology teaches that millions of years ago, life upon the earth was very simple, and that gradually more and more complex forms of life appeared, as the rocks formed latest in time show the most highly developed forms of animal life. The great English scientist, Charles Darwin, from this and other evidence, explained the theory of evolution. This is the belief that simple forms of life on the earth slowly and gradually gave rise to those more complex and that thus ultimately the most complex forms came into existence.

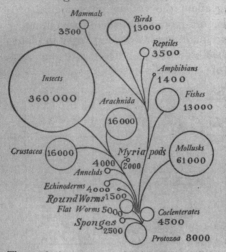

The evolutionary tree. Modified from Galloway. Copy this diagram in your notebook. Explain it as well as you can.

The Number of Animal Species. — Over 500,000 species of animals are known to exist to-day, as the following table shows.

Protozoa	8,000	Arachnids	16,000
Sponges	2,500	Crustaceans	16,000
Cœlenterates	4,500	Mollusks	61,000
Echinoderms	4,000	Fishes	13,000
Flatworms	5,000	Amphibians	1,400
Roundworms	1,500	Reptiles	3,500
Annelids	4,000	Birds	13,000
Insects	360,000	Mammals	3,500
Myriapods	2,000	Total	518,900

"How dared those scientists put man in a little ring like that with lions and tigers and everything that is bad?" Bryan demanded.

heard a block away. The microphones in the courtroom had no trouble picking up his speech.

"We do not need any experts," he announced. "The one beauty about the Word of God is, it does not take an expert to understand it."

In his long speech, Bryan repeatedly poked fun at science and those who abandoned their faith in religion. Like Darrow, he understood the power of humor. "The Christian believes man came from above, but the evolutionist believes he must have come from below," he said, to great laughter in the courtroom.

He flourished Hunter's *Civic Biology* in the air, declaiming, "There is the book they were teaching your children, that man was a mammal and so indistinguishable among the mammals!" He opened the book to the diagram that showed family trees of insects, reptiles, and other creatures, including man. He made fun of the fact that "man" wasn't even mentioned, just lumped in anonymously with all the other mammals. Darwin's theory of evolution meant that humans were no more special than dogs or horses. Bryan complained that the authors of the book "leave him [man] there with three thousand four hundred and ninety-nine other mammals, including elephants!" There was laughter and applause. "Tell me that the parents of this day have not any right to declare that children are not to be taught this doctrine!"

Bryan got a lot of laughs. But for some unknown reason, he did not bring up a serious argument that many people felt was the truly frightening thing about the teaching of evolution to young and impressionable minds—the idea known as Social Darwinism, which was based on Charles Darwin's concept of "the survival of the fittest."

Darwin observed that in nature some individual organisms are more fitted to survive than others—for example, one hawk might have longer wings or sharper talons than another, which would help it hunt more successfully. Therefore this hawk might survive where other, less "fit" hawks would die. The fittest organisms, Darwin argued, would be more likely to survive and reproduce. Darwin never claimed that one organism was better than others, only that some were more likely to survive.

But this concept led some social philosophers to suggest that perhaps some humans were more deserving of survival than others. The homeless, the poor, the mentally ill—they seemed to be less "fit" and therefore it was part of the natural order that they not survive.

George Hunter, the author of *Civic Biology*, agreed with these views, and when he wrote his textbook in 1914 he stated this idea in no uncertain terms. "If such people were lower animals, we would probably kill them off to prevent them from spreading."

Bryan had often argued forcefully against the dangers of Social Darwinism. He felt that it undermined the Christian ideal of charity to all. Taken to extremes, the ruthless principle of Social Darwinism could pave the way to eugenics: controlled selective breeding of humans to improve the overall population. It

HUNTER'S *CIVIC BIOLOGY*

—•—

Studies have been made on a number of different families in this country, in which mental and moral defects [alcoholism and "feeblemindedness"] were present in one or both of the original parents . . .

Hundreds of families such as those described above exist to-day, spreading disease, immorality, and crime to all parts of this country. The cost to society of such families is very severe. Just as certain animals or plants become parasitic on other plants or animals, these families have become parasitic on society. They not only do harm to others by corrupting, stealing, or spreading disease, but they are actually protected and cared for by the state out of public money. Largely for them the poorhouse and the asylum exist. They take from society, but they give nothing in return. They are true parasites.

could even lead to sterilization or execution of "inferior" humans. The text of *Civic Biology* enthusiastically recommended eugenics, and ominously foreshadows the fact that, in less than twenty years, the Nazis would carry Social Darwinism to ghastly extremes in their ghoulish quest to create a "master race."

Another powerful argument against teaching Darwinism was that white supremacists could claim that Darwin's theories led to the conclusion that some races of *Homo sapiens* were more evolved and therefore more "civilized" than others. Again, Hunter agreed, and his textbook stated that there were "five races or varieties of man, each very different from the other . . . These are the Ethiopian or negro type, originating in Africa; the Malay or brown race, from the islands of the Pacific; the American Indian; the Mongolian or yellow race, including the natives of China, Japan, and the Eskimos; and finally, the highest type of all, the Caucasians, represented by the civilized white inhabitants of Europe and America."

As the audience in the sweltering courtroom listened eagerly, Bryan went on with his speech, but he confined it to the religious arguments against evolution. He never mentioned eugenics or Social Darwinism during the trial, although he had often preached against them before. No one knows why he chose not to advance these powerful arguments. Perhaps he felt that his audience cared little for the larger social issues. He knew that they were fervent supporters of their traditional religious beliefs, founded on the words of the Bible.

And Bryan certainly delighted his audience. The crowd thoroughly enjoyed the speech, frequently calling out "Amen!" and laughing uproariously at the jokes. When Bryan finished, they ignored Raulston's warning—they clapped and cheered, as the floorboards creaked ominously.

Now the defense was in the last ditch. Their claim that evolution and the Bible did not contradict each other was the very last argument they had left. If the scientists weren't allowed to testify, John Scopes had

SCOPES

by W. E. B. Du Bois

Crisis Magazine: NAACP Newsletter, September 1925

The truth is and we know it, Dayton, Tennessee, is America: a great, ignorant, and simpleminded land, curiously compounded of brutality, bigotry, religious faith and demagoguery, and capable not simply of mistakes but of persecution, lynching, murder, and idiotic blundering as well as charity, missions, love and hope.

This is America and America is what it is because we believe in ignorance . . .

The folk who leave white Tennessee in blank and ridiculous ignorance of what science has taught the world since 1859 are the same ones who would leave black Tennessee and black America with just as little education as is consistent with fairly efficient labor and reasonable contentment; who rave over the 18th Amendment [prohibition of alcoholic beverages] and are dumb over the 15th [giving Black men the right to vote]; who permit lynching and make bastardy legal in order to render their race "pure." . . .

Dayton Tennessee is no laughing matter. It is menace and warning. It is a challenge to Religion, Science, and Democracy.

Dudley Field Malone wasn't as famous as some of the other lawyers, but his speech brought the house down—almost literally.

no hope at all of winning the case. But it wasn't the famous Clarence Darrow who rose to answer Bryan. Instead, the lawyer from Manhattan, Dudley Field Malone, stood up.

The rural southerners in the audience regarded the defense lawyers from northern cities like New York and Chicago with deep suspicion. Even the judge referred to them as "foreigners." Malone, however, had won some grudging respect from the local citizens by absolutely refusing to give in to the heat. Day after day, he had sat calmly in the baking courtroom, every button on his double-breasted suit buttoned up, his tie neatly tied. Now he slowly took off his coat, folded it carefully, and put it on the defense table. Then he turned to face the audience.

Malone made an unusual speech, which was long remembered by many who heard it. He raised a question that no one else had asked: What about the students? The trial was all about the older generation debating how to raise the youngsters. What if young people could be trusted to think for themselves?

"I would like to say something for the children of the country," Malone began. "We have no fears about the young people of America. They are a pretty smart generation . . . As a matter of fact, I feel that the children of this generation are probably much wiser than many of their elders."

Malone reminded the audience of the horrible carnage of World War I, ended only seven years earlier:

"We have just had a war with twenty million dead. Civilization is not so proud of the work of the adults . . . The least that this generation can do, Your Honor, is to give the next generation all the facts, all the available data, all the theories, all the information that learning, that study, that observations have produced—give it to the children in the hope of heaven that they will make a better world of this than we have been able to make it."

Fundamentalists like Bryan implored parents and teachers to shelter the innocent minds of children from dangerous ideas. But Malone begged, "For God's sake let the children have their minds kept open—close no doors to their knowledge; shut no door from them. Make the distinction between theology and science—let them have both!"

Malone had been a businesslike, low-key presence in the courtroom, but in this speech he let his passion show. He finished up with a ringing defense of each individual's freedom to speak and to hear the truth. "The truth always wins and we are not afraid of it. The truth is no coward. The truth does not need the law. The truth does not need the forces of government. The truth does not need Mr. Bryan . . . We are ready to tell the truth as we understand it and we do not fear all the truth that they can present as facts."

By now he was shouting at the top of his voice: "We feel we stand with fundamental freedom in America. We are not afraid. Where is the fear? We meet it! Where is the fear? We defy it!"

And then an amazing thing happened. The same listeners who had cheered Bryan's defense of the Bible rose to their feet and responded to Malone's plea for truth—with a burst of applause that literally shook the old courthouse to its foundations. They shouted, whistled, and stamped for many minutes as the judge pounded his gavel for order.

It was a far greater ovation than Bryan had received. It may have been an indication of the feelings of many of the spectators, even Bryan's ardent supporters, who were uneasy about suppressing the evidence of the scientists. If the trial was a "duel to the death," as Bryan had claimed, then it was hardly a fair duel if one side couldn't use any weapons. "And in the applauding," wrote a local reporter, "were many Daytonians who had come to scoff and left to think."

As the noise finally died down, the scientists sat patiently waiting. They had traveled hundreds of miles to testify, and were eager to explain to the jury, and to the world, what evolution was all about. They would plead that studying science did not have to mean the destruction of religion.

But they would never get a chance to speak. Judge Raulston ruled that expert scientific testimony would be "wholly irrelevant, incompetent and impertinent to the issues pending, and that it should be excluded."

The defense lawyers were furious. Darrow pounded the table with his fist, shouted, and protested until the judge threatened to have him jailed. But his protests were to no avail. The prosecutors were grinning and slapping each other on the back. Plainly, the case was as good as finished.

It was Friday afternoon, and the long, hot, dramatic week was over. Court was adjourned until Monday morning, when the last loose ends would be tied up.

Many of the journalists were personally on the side of the defense, and felt regretful at how things had turned out. "All that remains of the great cause of the State of Tennessee against the infidel Scopes is the formal business of bumping off the defendant," Mencken wrote bitterly. "There may be some legal jousting on Monday and some gaudy oratory on Tuesday, but the main battle is over, with Genesis completely triumphant."

John Scopes remembered the feeling of frustration and defeat as the defense team and the scientists trudged the dusty road back to the boardinghouse. The grand Monkey Trial, which was to teach the world about science and abolish an unjust law, had ended with a disappointing fizzle. The reporters, sick of sleeping on cots, eating hotel food, and spending long cramped hours in the hot courtroom, decided that the show was pretty much over. Most of them, including Mencken, packed their bags and left Dayton. By Monday morning only a handful remained.

But the Monkey Trial wasn't quite over yet. "It was as though the sportswriters had left a ball game at the seventh inning stretch," John remembered. "There was a lot of trial left."

Chapter Eight

"The Evening and the Morning Were the First Day"

A DELIGHTFULLY COOL breeze rustled the leaves of the big maple and oak trees on the courthouse lawn. John Scopes was still on trial, but at least the setting was more agreeable. Fearing that the courthouse foundations would collapse under the strain of so many people, Judge Raulston had announced on Monday morning that the trial would resume outdoors.

Chairs and tables were hastily set up on a large wooden speaker's platform on the shady courthouse lawn. Several hundred people sat on benches, watching the proceedings. The huge READ YOUR BIBLE sign loomed over the platform. The defense protested, and after

Huge maple trees provided a cool archway over the open-air stage.

some argument, the banner was taken down.

Over the weekend, the scientists had written out their statements on evolution so that their testimony would be in the official record, since the case was likely to be appealed. Arthur Hays read these affidavits aloud for more than two hours, but no one paid much attention. His droning voice, describing the details of evolutionary theory, made many people drowsy. Local kids sold soda pop and lemonade to the audience, and as the afternoon wore on, the crowd thinned. More reporters quietly left.

Hays finally finished the scientific testimony, and everyone expected that now the defense would rest its case. But there was one more witness to be called.

Clarence Darrow had come up with a shocking idea. He had discussed it on the weekend with a few of the team behind closed doors, but not even the defendant knew what was going to come next. "Watch out," Malone, who was in on the secret, murmured to Scopes. "Hell is going to pop now."

In his quiet voice, Hays announced, "The defense desires to call Mr. Bryan as a witness."

Everyone woke up at that. John remembered the scene: "All of the lawyers leaped to their feet at once. The judge blanched and was at a loss for words. Everyone seemed to be talking at once." It was almost unheard of for the defense to call a member of the prosecution as a witness. Bryan was being called as an expert witness—not on the subject of evolution, but on the Bible.

Tom Stewart protested loudly, and the other prosecutors joined in. But they were abruptly overruled by William Jennings Bryan himself. Bryan announced that he was eager to be called as a witness to the truth of the Holy Scriptures.

By this point in the trial, both Darrow and Bryan were deeply frustrated. Both men burned to show the justice of their cause. Darrow wanted to make a statement about the dangers of religion banning science that would be heard around the world. Bryan wanted to preach his own message far and wide, and he was exasperated with the way Tom Stewart had kept the case to a narrow legal focus.

As Bryan took his seat on the witness chair, word spread along the streets of Dayton. People hurried over to watch the fun. Soon more than three thousand spectators were crammed tightly around the platform. Some stood on the hoods of nearby parked cars; others hung out of courthouse windows or crowded in the dusty streets. About the only people in town who didn't join the audience were the twelve angry jurymen, still barred from attending. Almost everyone else in Dayton watched the confrontation between Darwinism's most famous defender and its bitterest foe.

Darrow stood in his shirtsleeves on the platform, head thrust forward at Bryan, who was fanning himself vigorously. "You have given considerable study to the Bible, haven't you, Mr. Bryan?" Darrow asked politely.

"Yes, sir, I have tried to," Bryan replied.

"Do you claim that everything in the Bible should be literally interpreted?"

"I believe everything in the Bible should be accepted as it is given there."

Darrow started off in a casual, relaxed manner, but he was well prepared. He had spent Sunday secretly rehearsing this examination, with one of the scientists acting as Bryan. They had planned some tough questions. Darrow had been thinking about some of these questions for years. He had posed them to Bryan once before, during their duel in the newspapers, and Bryan had refused even to consider them. But now he was under oath to answer to the best of his ability.

The showdown between Darrow and Bryan lasted two hours.

Darrow never brought up Darwin, or evolution, or monkeys. He also steered clear of the miracles of Jesus in the New Testament. Instead, he stuck to the miraculous events of the Old Testament, popular Sunday school stories such as Noah's Ark. "You believe the story of the Flood to be a literal interpretation?" he asked.

"Yes, sir."

"When was that flood?" Darrow inquired. "About four thousand and four BC?"

This was not an idle question. One of the major controversies between science and Fundamentalism was on the age of the earth. Although most scientists had long accepted that the planet is billions of years old, Fundamentalist biblical scholars disagreed. By counting back through the generations of people listed in the Bible, they had fixed the dates of the Flood, and of Creation itself.

Bryan was cautious, wary of a trap. "That has been the estimate . . . I would not say it is accurate."

"But what do you think that the Bible itself says? Don't you know how it [that date] was arrived at?" Bryan had to admit that he didn't know the method used to arrive at that precise date. "But what do you think?" Darrow persisted.

Bryan was at a loss. "I do not think about . . . things I don't think about."

Darrow shot back, "Do you think about things you do think about?"

"Well, sometimes," Bryan said.

A roar of laughter swept through the crowd. "Let us have order!" the judge called, as Bryan looked out at a sight he had never seen before: a crowd of thousands laughing—not at his jokes, but at him.

Oddly, one of the few who didn't burst into laughter was John Scopes, sitting quietly off to the side. He remembered the day six years before when he had giggled out loud at Bryan's speech. Now he felt pity for the perspiring old man trapped on the witness chair, being hammered by Darrow's interrogation.

Bryan grew ever more rattled as Darrow continued, firing dozens of questions in rapid succession. Bryan testified that the Flood had wiped out all human life on earth, excepting only Noah and his family. Since the edition of the Holy Bible that Tom Stewart had presented as evidence stated in an afterword that the Flood had occurred in exactly 2348 BCE, this meant that Bryan was denying the existence of any cultures, like those of ancient Egypt or China, that stretched back more than four thousand years.

Darrow peppered Bryan with questions on a variety of topics: historic civilizations, fossil layers, ancient languages. Over the course of two hours, Bryan was forced to admit his ignorance of history, archeology, geology, and biology, and had to reply, "I don't know" . . . "I can't say" . . . "I'm not sure." In spite of the cool shade, the questions and answers were growing more heated and tense. Stewart objected repeatedly, but each time, Bryan insisted he wanted to continue.

Darrow kept up the pace, driving Bryan off-balance with questions about hard-to-believe Bible stories: Did a whale really swallow Jonah and spit him out after three days? Could Joshua make the sun stand still in the sky? Was Eve literally created out of Adam's rib? And then Darrow asked the trickiest question of all: "Do you think the earth was made in six days?"

"Not six days of twenty-four hours," Bryan replied. There was a shocked gasp from the audience.

Bryan had fallen into Darrow's trap—he had admitted there might possibly be a word in the Bible that did not have to be taken literally. This was a huge admission. If a biblical day wasn't literally twenty-four hours, could it be twenty-five hours? Or a hundred hours? Could a "day" refer to a vast period of geologic time, millions of years long?

Darrow swiftly followed up his advantage. He

brought up the point that according to Genesis, God did not create the sun until the fourth day. So how to tell if precisely twenty-four hours had passed? When Darrow, scenting victory, pressed Bryan on how long the first "day" was, Bryan repeated, "I do not think it means necessarily a twenty-four-hour day."

"What do you consider it to be?" Darrow persisted.

"I have not attempted to explain it," Bryan replied.

Once again Tom Stewart objected, demanding to know the purpose of these random questions. But Bryan refused to give up. "The only purpose Mr. Darrow has is to slur at the Bible," he roared, jumping to his feet, "but I will answer his questions!"

"I object to your statement," Darrow shouted back. "I am examining you on your fool ideas that no intelligent Christian on earth believes!" The two opponents were standing almost toe-to-toe, red-faced and glaring, shaking their fists at each other.

Judge Raulston finally decided it was time to call it quits. He abruptly announced that court was adjourned for the day.

Darrow was immediately surrounded by an admiring crowd: lawyers and scientists, reporters and Dayton businessmen, all congratulating him, shaking his hand, begging for an interview. The audience began to disperse, some thoughtful, some angry, some chatting and laughing. Bryan sat slumped in the witness chair, exhausted and alone.

Anita Sanchez

THE INSTANT JUDGE RAULSTON banged his
gavel, reporters jumped up and sprinted for the "Press
Hall." This was what the journalists called the stuffy loft
over Bailey's Hardware Store, where their desks, typewriters, and sleeping cots were located.

John Scopes panted along after the reporters. He
had made friends with several of them, and was eager to help get the story out. They spent the evening
writing their accounts of the dramatic confrontation.
John wrote out his version in longhand, lament-
ing that he couldn't keep up with the reporters who
pounded furiously on their typewriters. Delighted
that they had scooped their rivals who had left town
early, the few remaining reporters wired their stories
to New York, Baltimore, Chicago, St. Louis, and cities
across the country.

The Monkey Trial's grand battle was front-page
news everywhere. Newspapers across the nation re-
printed excerpts from Darrow's examination of Bryan.
One editor wrote, "It has brought about a striking revelation of the Fundamentalist mind in all its shallow
depth and narrow intolerance." Darrow's jokes and
Bryan's lame answers were repeated many times: *Do
you ever think about things you do think about? Well,
sometimes* . . .

In the court of public opinion, the verdict seemed
clear. John Scopes—and science—had won.

But the trial still wasn't over.

THE NEXT MORNING was rainy, so the court moved back indoors. Little remained to be done. All the witnesses had been called, all the shouting was over.

At the end of a trial, both the prosecution and the defense usually make closing statements, summing up all their best arguments to persuade the jury. William Jennings Bryan had come to court that morning carrying a thick sheaf of papers—his final speech, which he had been perfecting for weeks. But Clarence Darrow had one last trick up his sleeve.

"I think, to save time," Darrow said casually, "we will ask the court to bring in the jury." This meant that the case would immediately go to the jury, and no defense lawyer would make a final speech—but that meant the prosecution couldn't speak either. Tom Stewart, realizing the damage Bryan had done to his case, quickly agreed. Bryan was denied his chance to make the triumphant oration that he had hoped would be the peak of his career.

The long-suffering jury members were finally allowed back into the courtroom, but they hardly had time to sit down before they were sent out again, this time to consider their verdict. The jurymen pushed through the crowd and huddled in the hallway, where they conferred briefly. They returned in less than ten minutes.

Head bowed, the teacher stood in front of the judge's bench. John was exhausted, and his tired face showed it. "Mr. Scopes, the jury has found you guilty under this indictment," Raulston said. "The court now

fixes your fine at one hundred dollars and imposes that fine upon you—"

"May it please Your Honor!" John Neal interrupted. "We want to be heard a moment." Neal reminded the judge that the defendant had to be given an opportunity to speak before sentence was passed.

Embarrassed at his mistake, the judge stammered, "Oh, have you anything to say, Mr. Scopes, as to why the court should not impose punishment upon you?"

John was as startled as the judge. No one had mentioned that he should prepare a statement. He thought for a moment, then said quietly, "Your Honor, I feel that I have been convicted of violating an unjust statute. I will continue in the future, as I have in the past, to oppose this law in any way I can."

After sentencing, the last odds and ends were tidied up. The defense filed a Notice of Appeal. The lawyers

The teacher standing before the judge.

formally thanked the court. Raulston replied with a mini-sermon on "the indestructability" of the Word of God, making it clear once again which side he was on. And Arthur Hays got the last good laugh of the trial by offering the judge a copy of Darwin's *On the Origin of Species* as a parting gift.

John felt a huge surge of relief as the proceedings slowly wound to an end. "I was free of courtroom drama!" he wrote later. "I could indulge myself in privacy and could even swim straight through the lunch hour and all afternoon if I wished." After a brief closing prayer, the judge banged his gavel for the last time, and the Monkey Trial was over.

Only it wasn't.

Chapter Nine

The Circus Leaves Town

"WHEN A CIRCUS leaves town, there are always the tents to move and the wagons to load and the debris that must be cleaned up," John remembered. "That was the way it was in Dayton."

The READ YOUR BIBLE signs were taken down. Lemonade stands went out of business. Monkeys disappeared. Thousands of visitors who had flooded into Dayton trickled away: lawyers, journalists, evangelists, sightseers. John was sorry to part with some of the reporters who had become his friends. He helped carry their bags to the train station and waved farewell as the train pulled out. Clarence Darrow left for a vacation in the cool hill country. Soon, John wrote, "Dayton was once again its old deserted self." The one principal figure of the trial who remained in town was William Jennings Bryan, rewriting his undelivered speech as a newspaper article.

Right away, John began to make plans for a future that wouldn't involve any mention of monkeys. Three days after the trial ended, he took a trip to visit the University of Kentucky, to see about going back to college. Inspired by the fascinating debates of the scientists who had stayed in the "Monkey House," he was considering a degree in geology.

At the train station on his way home, John was astonished to see a pack of the reporters he had so recently bidden farewell to, all boarding the train back to Dayton. "What happened?" he demanded.

"Bryan died a few hours ago!" a reporter told him. Five days after the trial had ended, Bryan had gone to bed for a midday nap and never woken up.

Bryan's death, coming dramatically soon after the end of the trial, gave him back much of the prestige he had lost after his confrontation with Darrow. Huge rallies were held in many cities, as thousands mourned their hero under enormous flag-draped images of his face. The governor of Tennessee issued a proclamation declaring Bryan's funeral a state holiday, adding that Bryan had died a martyr's death.

Bryan's last speech was printed posthumously in many newspapers. His undelivered message was like words spoken from the grave, imploring Christians to

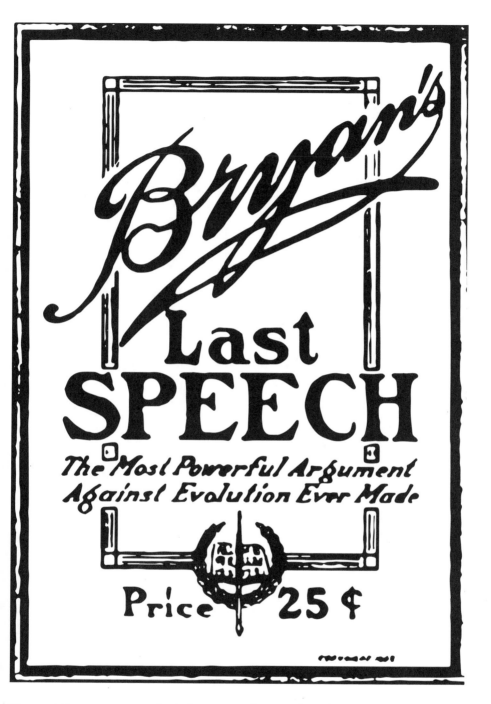

The speech Bryan never got to give in the courtroom became a bestseller after his sudden death.

carry on the sacred cause of defending the Bible. Country music balladeers wrote songs about his glorious last battle:

He fought the evolutionists and infidel men, fools
Who are trying to ruin the minds of children in our
schools . . .

The cause of Bryan's sudden death is unknown. He was sixty-five years old, diabetic, and had undoubtedly been stressed by the days of terrible heat. But many Bryan supporters blamed his death squarely on Clarence Darrow. "Why, that man's got horns, I tell you!" one Daytonite told John in a furious rant against Darrow. "He's got the horns of the devil."

In spite of the frenzy of mourning for Bryan, there were no more Monkey Trials. Many newspapers and radio broadcasters had been brutally critical of the goings-on in Dayton, and no state wanted to be held up to national mockery the way Tennessee had been. Headlines like "Cranks and Freaks Flock to Dayton" in the *New York Times* were typical of many big-city articles on the Monkey Trial. Mencken's widely read editorials had heaped scorn on the rural folk of the South, repeatedly insulting them as boobs, yokels, and ignoramuses.

Nineteen states were considering anti-evolution laws, but during the next few years, only two states, Mississippi and Arkansas, actually passed such laws. As soon as the topic was raised in any state's legislature, there was immediate, furious controversy—and lots and lots of publicity. After the Monkey Trial, it was impossible to pass anti-evolution legislation with little public debate, as had happened with the Butler Act.

Although scientific testimony had been suppressed during the trial, the vast publicity in newspapers, radio, and newsreels ensured that practically no American could avoid learning about evolution, whether they wanted to or not. The national biology lesson had been taught, after all. Professor Fay-Cooper Cole, one of the scientists who had not been allowed to testify, wrote,

The two books that were at the center of the storm.

"Where one person had been interested in evolution before the trial, scores were reading and inquiring at its close."

John Scopes's case wasn't finished. The legal process marched on, although much more slowly than it had that feverish spring, when John's trial was scheduled only a few weeks after his arrest. The case was appealed immediately, but the Tennessee Supreme Court reviewed it almost a year later and did not reach a decision until 1927. (To John's delight, his attendance at the hearings was not necessary.) Keenly sensitive to the ridicule heaped on their state, Tennessee's elected officials were anxious to have the case go quietly away with no more embarrassing "monkey" headlines. The Tennessee Supreme Court judges overturned the verdict on a technical point of law that somehow all the defense lawyers had missed: legally, the exact amount of the fine should have been set by the jury, not the judge.

The State of Tennessee v. John Thomas Scopes was dismissed with little fanfare or public notice. John was officially declared innocent. This quiet victory was actually a huge defeat for Scopes, Darrow, and the ACLU: It meant that the appeal could not advance to the United States Supreme Court, and the attempt to overturn the anti-evolution law was dead in the water. The Butler Act remained in force.

But the controversy over evolution was raging more fiercely than ever.

To students like Howard Morgan and Bud Shelton, evolution hadn't been a controversial issue. It was just another part of a dull biology lesson—they memorized a few key points for a test, then quickly forgot them. But after the Monkey Trial, "evolution" had become a national battlefield. For many Americans, defending or condemning Darwin's theories became, as Bryan had put it, "a duel to the death."

Judge Raulston's decision to exclude scientific testimony meant that compromise was ignored—not only during the trial, but in its aftermath. The voices of highly educated professors who were also devoutly religious had not been heard; the idea that evolution was a process created by God was rarely considered. The evolution conflict seemed to have two sides, and two sides only. Small room for middle ground.

The Monkey Trial polarized the nation. The participation of big-city lawyers like Darrow and Malone, and the invasion by urban reporters into a small rural town encouraged a growing sense of "us versus them," pitting country folk against city-dwellers. Mencken's insults rankled, and Fundamentalists began to think of evolutionists as an "elite" who despised those less educated. Pro-evolutionists often saw "antis" as ignorant bigots who wanted to bring education back to the Middle Ages. In 1925, the Civil War was long over, but the tragic, bloody conflict was still a living memory for many southerners, and the Scopes trial ripped open unhealed wounds, once again setting North against

South. The very word "evolution" had become a magic spell that summoned painful emotions of anger, fear, and hate.

NEITHER SIDE WANTED another circus with superstar lawyers and capering monkeys. But Fundamentalists quickly realized that there were other ways to nudge evolution out of the classroom.

When William Jennings Bryan had begun his crusade, textbooks across the nation had included evolution as an accepted part of science. Bryan had complained that he could not "find any text book on biology which does not begin with monkeys." As soon as the Scopes trial ended, that began to change.

George Hunter, the author of *Civic Biology*, made alterations to his now-world-famous book in an attempt to make it less controversial and not lose sales. The original text had been enthusiastic about the "wonderful discovery of the doctrine of evolution," and hailed Darwin as "the great English scientist." Now Hunter removed every reference to evolution, substituting the word "development." But the cuts were in vain—the state of Tennessee canceled all use of Hunter's *Civic Biology* anyway.

A few months after the trial, the governor of Texas ordered that references to evolution be cut from all schoolbooks. If any Texas public schools wanted to keep the books they already had, the offending paragraphs had to be literally cut out—with scissors.

In the years that followed, more and more states refused to buy textbooks that mentioned evolution. To keep from going bankrupt, virtually all textbook companies diluted or removed references to evolution. A few texts hid the controversial material in the appendix, listing the "Theory of Evolution" as one of several theories that were unproven. Teachers who said the "E-word" in the classroom risked losing their jobs. A national survey taken in 1940 indicated that approximately half of all high school science teachers did not even mention evolution in their courses.

But in the 1950s, things began to change again. Darwin was brought back to life more than thirty years after the Monkey Trial, by the unlikely event of a Russian satellite hurtling through space.

In 1957, the Soviet Union and the United States were mired deep in the Cold War, both superpowers vying with each other to be first and best in science and technology. When Russia's Sputnik satellite was the first to orbit earth, it sent a chill down many American spines. If the Soviets could defeat America in space, what else could they do? Russian high school students routinely studied five years of in-depth biology, chemistry, and physics. Science education in America was in for a complete overhaul.

Congress swiftly passed national legislation encouraging education in the sciences for all grade levels. In 1961, the American Institute of Biological Sciences released a series of textbooks returning evolution to its place as the cornerstone of biology. These books were used in states across the nation, including Arkansas, Mississippi, and Tennessee—states that still had laws in place banning the teaching of evolution.

In 1967, a Tennessee parent filed a lawsuit in the name of his fourteen-year-old son Thomas Southern, claiming that the boy's right to an education was being limited, and demanding that the Butler Act be overturned. Fearing another Monkey Trial, Tennessee legislators introduced a bill to finally repeal the famous act.

Once again, the "Monkey Law" attracted violent emotion, drama, and comedy. As the bill was noisily debated in the Tennessee state capitol, reporters packed the hall, and television cameras recorded the furious debate. At one point, opponents carried in a caged monkey with a sign that read HELLO, DADDY-O!

It seemed like the Scopes trial was still going on. The same arguments about corrupting the morals of children were raised, with the same passion: "We will bring chaos to the hearts and minds of the young if they believe they are just another type of animal." Many legislators argued that voting to overturn the anti-evolution law would equal denying their faith in Jesus. One representative said, "I have no hope of life after death if I accept this theory [of evolution.] I must cling to faith." As television cameras recorded the tense vote, the Butler Act was upheld on a tie.

But the drama still wasn't over. A few months later, in a small-town Tennessee classroom, a twenty-four-year-old high school biology teacher taught a class on evolution. Unlike John Scopes, Gary Scott wasn't arrested, but he did get fired. With the support of the ACLU, the National Education Association, and the National Science Teachers Association, he went to court. The media immediately began referring to his case as "Scopes II."

Three days after Gary Scott filed his lawsuit against the state, the Tennessee legislature repealed the Butler Act.

Epilogue

ON A SULTRY July afternoon, John Scopes walked down the main street of Dayton, past Doc Robinson's Drug Store. The sidewalks were crowded with sightseers and tourists from all over the country. But this was thirty-five years after the trial that made Dayton famous, and many things had changed. Gone were the elm-shaded dirt roads, the horse-drawn wagons and Model-T Fords. The busy streets were all paved now, and filled with Chevrolets and Buicks. But the weather was the same, as hot and sticky as ever.

John had returned to Tennessee in 1960 by special invitation from a Hollywood movie studio. Dayton was hosting the world premiere of *Inherit the Wind*, a film based on an award-winning Broadway play that dramatized the events of those hot July days so long ago. Posters on the walls of the theater proclaimed, IT'S ALL ABOUT THE FABULOUS MONKEY TRIAL THAT ROCKED AMERICA!

John was now fifty-nine years old, but the trial was still a vivid memory. He saw few familiar faces on the crowded Dayton streets, though. Most of the participants in the Monkey Trial had long since passed away, and were all but forgotten. William Jennings Bryan was no longer a household name across America. After the Scopes trial, Clarence Darrow teamed up once again with the ACLU attorney Arthur Garfield Hays and successfully defended a Black doctor who had been charged with murder, but Darrow had died in 1938. Judge Raulston, the acidic reporter H. L. Mencken, and most of the jurymen had long since passed away. John's teenage students, like Howard Morgan and Bud Shelton, were now men in their forties and fifties who had mostly moved away to seek jobs in bigger towns.

This was John's first visit back to Tennessee in decades. After the trial, John knew he didn't want to teach in Dayton anymore—especially since the school board would require him to sign a pledge not to mention evolution. He could have cashed in on his nationwide fame and been set for life. During the trial he had received so much mail that the town had hired a special postman just for him. From all over the world, people sent John scoldings, sermons, curses, congratulations, marriage proposals, and job offers, including a $50,000 offer to lecture on evolution as part of a vaudeville act. A few days after the trial ended, he piled up the mountainous heap of mail, with most of the letters unopened, and lit a bonfire.

John had been a spellbound audience member during the scientific debates in the Monkey House, and a participant, too. The scientists appreciated his keen interest, and several of them arranged a scholarship for him at the University of Chicago. He enjoyed the peace and quiet of the library and the laboratory, and was usually successful at dodging pesky reporters who still wanted to interview him. Just as the scholarship money was running low, he was thrilled to receive a fellowship— money that would enable him to complete his PhD. But abruptly, he received a letter from the president of the university, informing him that the fellowship money was no longer available to him. The letter read, "Your name has been removed from consideration for the fellowship. As far as I am concerned, you can take your atheistic marbles and play elsewhere."

"Notoriety," John wrote with bitterness, "is as tenacious as a bedbug." He realized that the famous trial would always be "the monkey on my back." So he decided to get about as far as he could from anyone who had heard of the "Trial of the Century." He accepted a job with an oil company to work as an exploratory geologist in the remote rainforests of Venezuela.

John returned to the USA after years abroad,

married, had children, and continued working as a geologist. As the decades passed, his children grew up and his sandy hair turned gray. And people finally began to forget about the Monkey Trial. Until a hit Broadway play, and then a movie, brought it all back to life.

John wandered around the town, reliving old memories. He paused in front of the courthouse to read a historical marker explaining the trial. When he got thirsty, he headed to Doc Robinson's Drug Store for a cool drink. It was still a popular spot, but there were no more "Simian Sundaes." Instead, to celebrate the movie opening, "Scopes Sodas" were for sale.

There was one big change that John noted—Rhea Central High School, where John had made history that April morning, wasn't there anymore. In 1930, the school had moved to a new location, and the building had been turned into William Jennings Bryan College, dedicated to teaching Fundamentalist Christian principles.

Since its beginning days with only thirty students, Bryan College has become a thriving institution with more than 1,400 students. All staff (though not students) must annually sign a statement of belief, affirming that "all humanity is descended from Adam and Eve. They are historical persons created by God in a special formative act, and not from previously existing life forms."

The anti-evolution movement is stronger today than it was in 1925. Legally, however, Fundamentalists have suffered many setbacks. In 1968, a case about the teaching of evolution finally reached the United States Supreme Court. An Arkansas teacher named Susan Epperson had sued the state to have its anti-evolution law overturned. The Supreme Court struck down the Arkansas law as unconstitutional.

Susan Epperson, the science teacher whose case against the anti-evolution law finally made it to the Supreme Court.

But the war over evolution has raged on through the decades, growing more heated, not less.

In many states, Fundamentalists have introduced a topic called creation science, insisting that it be taught alongside evolution. A similar concept is intelligent design. This is the theory that the creation of the world was guided by an intelligent cause—God—and that living organisms could not be the result of the random

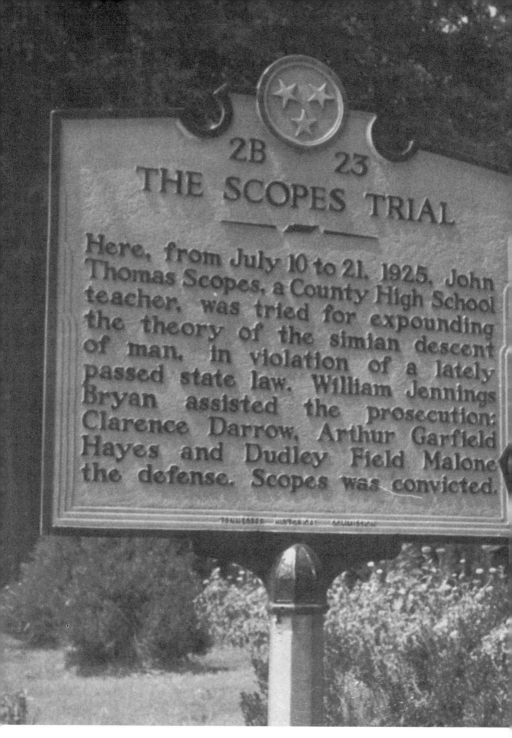

John Scopes in front of the historical marker explaining the "Monkey Trial."

process of natural selection. Often, Fundamentalists downplay the religious basis of these concepts, not referring to the Bible or to God, and present them as valid science.

Again and again, attempts to force teachers to teach alternatives to evolution were found to be unconstitutional, since these concepts are part of a religion, not science. In 1975, a Tennessee law that required textbooks to include creationism was struck down, and similar laws in Arkansas and Louisiana were also rejected by the Supreme Court in the 1980s. In 2005, a Pennsylvania school district tried and failed to require teachers to present intelligent design as an alternative theory to balance the teaching of evolution. And the issue keeps resurfacing, with laws allowing the teaching of creationism being proposed in school districts and state legislatures almost every year.

Whether or not Darwin maintains his place in the classroom and the textbooks, millions of people today believe evolution is a myth. A 2019 Gallup Poll found that 40 percent of Americans believe that God created humans in their present form, and do not agree with Darwin's Theory of Evolution. In the twenty-first century, the Scopes case is still not over, as the battle over evolution continues, constantly and relentlessly calling science into doubt.

Today, millions of people who do not believe in evolution also refuse to believe in the effectiveness of vaccines to cure disease. People disbelieve scientists who present evidence of catastrophic climate change threatening our planet. The Fundamentalist attack on evolution sowed a deep-rooted suspicion and mistrust of science that has spread to affect every part of national life.

IN THE DARKENED movie theater, John Scopes watched the Hollywood version of his life on the silver screen. "I enjoyed the movie," he commented afterward. He especially got a kick out of watching Dick York, the handsome movie star who played the role of the teacher.

Inherit the Wind wasn't meant to be a documentary, and it made a lot of things different. The townspeople were threatening and violent. The teacher had a romance with a minister's beautiful daughter. And the Bryan character died in the courtroom at the end of the trial, dramatically clutching his chest and crashing to the floor. In the movie version, there was no doubt that the defense won the day. Spencer Tracy was nominated for an Oscar for his role as the lovable, eloquent defense lawyer.

But one thing the movie got right, John remembered. "The movie captured the emotions," he said, referring to the anger, hate, and suspicion aroused on both sides by the famous Monkey Trial. Those passions continue today as the culture wars rage harder than ever.

Who won the Monkey Trial?

The jury is still out.

AUTHOR'S NOTE

For some writers of history, the problem is finding information. But when I began to research the Scopes trial, I soon discovered that there was no lack of information—I was buried in it. The trial was covered by more than two hundred reporters, who collectively wrote more than two million words about the trial, the town, and the people in it. Every minute of the trial from the opening prayer to the final bang of the judge's gavel was recorded by the court stenographer, and preserved in a book that's about three inches thick. And hundreds of photographs and moving pictures were taken in Dayton during the spring and summer of 1925.

My problem was to bring all this mass of material to life. I wanted to turn the black-and-white images into a world of color and movement. I hoped to make those printed words come alive with the voices that shouted them. My goal was to try to recreate what Dayton looked like, sounded like, and even smelled like during that hot July so long ago.

To make any story vivid, a writer has to get inside the minds of the characters. In deciding how to present this tale, I wondered who the main character should be. Clarence Darrow? William Jennings Bryan? Howard Morgan? I finally found my hero in a teacher: John Scopes, a quiet person who hated the thought of notoriety but was willing to stand up for what he thought was right.

I wasn't writing fiction, so I couldn't make up people's words and emotions. All the dialog in quotation marks is taken word for word from the trial transcript, newspapers, or other writings. All the emotions were described by the people who felt them. For example, I was able to write that John felt nervous when he entered the courtroom, because he wrote in his memoirs that he felt nervous when entering the courtroom. Fortunately for me, John Scopes wrote a wonderful autobiography that preserves the flavor of the times, right down to the delicious sodas in Doc Robinson's drugstore.

In fiction, there is often a hero and a villain. But in real life it's rarely that simple. I was astonished to find that William Jennings Bryan, with whom I disagreed on evolution, was a huge supporter of a cause very dear to my heart: women's rights. And while H. L. Mencken's jokes made me chuckle, I found myself becoming outraged over his constant insulting of people who disagreed with him as "morons" and "yokels." That's no way to change people's minds.

Oddly enough, I finished writing this book during another long, hot, tense July: the first summer of the COVID-19 global pandemic. As I watched news reports of millions of people refusing to listen to the evidence put forth by scientists, I knew that the Monkey Trial was far from over.

The best journalists in that stifling courtroom tried to present the facts, reporting accurately what both sides had to say. So I have tried to do that—to tell both sides as fairly and honestly as I could. In the end, I agree with Dudley Field Malone that the young people of this country are pretty smart. And perfectly capable of making up their own minds about what they believe.

Glossary of Legal Terms

appeal: a process in which decisions in a court are reviewed by a higher court. The decision of the higher court can sometimes be appealed to an even higher court. The highest court in the nation is the United States Supreme Court.

attorney: a lawyer who has passed the state bar exam and is approved to practice law.

bail: a fee set by a judge to ensure that an accused person shows up for their trial. After paying bail, the accused person is free to go until the trial. The money will be reimbursed as long as they appear at the trial.

defendant: a person accused of committing a crime.

district attorney: an official in charge of prosecuting crimes on behalf of the state in a particular area, such as a county or city. In Tennessee, district attorneys are chosen by public election.

felony: a serious crime. Crimes like rape, kidnapping, arson, or murder are usually felonies.

grand jury: a group of citizens who listen to evidence presented by the prosecutors and determine whether it is reasonable to believe an individual committed a crime. If the grand jury finds that it is reasonable to believe that a crime has been committed, they will issue an indictment.

indictment: a grand jury's formal accusation of a serious crime. After a person is indicted, they stand trial. The prosecutor must prove beyond a reasonable doubt that the person is guilty of the crime.

jury: a group of people (usually twelve) who hear evidence in a trial and provide a verdict of guilty or not guilty.

misdemeanor: a crime less serious than a felony. Nonviolent, minor crimes like shoplifting are usually misdemeanors.

prosecutor: a legal official who conducts the case against a defendant in a court.

testimony: spoken or written statements given under oath during a trial.

verdict: a jury's decision.

voir dire: the process of selecting a jury. Prospective jurors are randomly selected from the local citizens, and questioned by the judge and/or both the defense and the prosecution to see if they can be fair and impartial.

AN EVOLUTIONARY TIME LINE

1859
Publication of Charles Darwin's
On the Origin of Species.

1871
Publication of Darwin's
The Descent of Man.

AN EVOLUTIONARY TIME LINE

1910

Publication of *The Fundamentals,* a series of booklets by conservative Protestant leaders, emphasizing the importance of taking the Bible literally. Publication is funded anonymously by two businessmen, Lyman and Milton Stewart, owners of the Standard Oil Company, and three million copies are distributed worldwide.

1919

First convention of World's Christian Fundamentals Association. More than 6,000 people attend. Anti-evolutionism becomes a central issue for Fundamentalists.

1915

The Ku Klux Klan re-founded with an agenda that includes education issues.

1923

Oklahoma passes a law providing free textbooks to schools, as long as the textbooks do not teach evolution

1914

Hunter's *Civic Biology* published.

1924

North Carolina Board of Education removes textbooks that discuss evolution from their list of approved textbooks.

1925

MARCH 21
Tennessee's Butler Anti-Evolution Act signed into law by Governor Peay.

APRIL 21
John Scopes teaches science class using *Civic Biology* (some witnesses remembered different dates).

MAY 5
John Scopes arrested.

MAY 25
Grand jury indictment of Scopes.

AN EVOLUTIONARY TIME LINE

JULY 10
Trial starts.

JULY 18
American Feder-
ation of Teachers
adopts resolution
condemning in-
tolerance and sup-
porting academic
freedom.

JULY 21
John Scopes found
guilty, trial ends.

JULY 26
Death of W
Jennings B

1926

Anti-evolution law
passes in Mississippi.

1928

Anti-evolution law
passes in Arkansas.

1927

Tennessee Supreme Court
overturns Scopes verdict
on a technicality, and the
case is dismissed.

1930

Bryan College opens to
teach Christian Funda-
mentalist principles.

AN EVOLUTIONARY TIME LINE

1955

Inherit the Wind, a play by Jerome Lawrence and Robert E. Lee, opens and is a hit on Broadway. The play is a fictional version of the Scopes trial.

1961

American Institute of Biological Sciences releases a series of textbooks emphasizing the importance of evolution in understanding biology.

1960

Inherit the Wind movie premiere. John Scopes revisits Dayton and is given the key to the city.

1968

Susan Epperson v. Arkansas. The Supreme Court unanimously declares unconstitutional a law banning the teaching of evolution in Arkansas public schools.

1967

APRIL 13

Tennessee teacher Gary Scott fired for teaching evolution.

MAY 15

Scott, with the support of ACLU and NSTA, files suit in federal court to overturn the Butler Act.

MAY 18

Tennessee state legislature repeals the Butler Act.

AN EVOLUTIONARY TIME LINE

2004

A Pennsylvania school board votes to require a description of intelligent design in its high school biology curriculum, but it is struck down as unconstitutional in 2005.

1987

Edwards v. Aguillard. The Supreme Court strikes down a Louisiana law requiring public schools to teach "creation science" alongside evolution.

2001

Congressman Rick Santorum proposes an amendment to the No Child Left Behind education reform bill, to ensure biology curricula mention alternatives to Darwinism. The amendment is removed before final passage of the bill after nationwide protests from scientists and educators.

2012

The National Center for Science Education, which fights the teaching of creationism, announces that it will battle climate change denial as well.

2007

The Creation Museum opens in Petersburg, Kentucky, operated by the Christian organization Answers in Genesis. It promotes a "young Earth" creationist explanation of the origin of the world.

2014

Bill Nye, famous as television's "The Science Guy," publicly debates Ken Ham, founder and CEO of Answers in Genesis, on the topic of evolution. An estimated three million viewers watch online.

AN EVOLUTIONARY TIME LINE

2019

Laws requiring schools to teach various theories about the origin of life, including creationism, are proposed in Indiana and South Carolina.

A Gallup Poll shows that 40 percent of adult Americans believe in "a strictly creationist view of human origins, believing that God created them in their present form within roughly the past 10,000 years."

And then . . . ?

Source Notes

INTRODUCTION: "CALL HOWARD MORGAN TO THE STAND"

2. "Your name is Howard": Horvath,
Transcript, p. 205.

1. "JOHN, WOULD YOU BE WILLING TO STAND FOR A TEST CASE?"

10. "teach any theory": The Butler Act as quoted in Larson,
Summer for the Gods, p. 50.

11. "Mr. Scopes? Mr. Robinson says": Scopes and Presley,
Center of the Storm, p. 57.

15. "Mr. Robinson, you": Larson, *Summer for the Gods*,
p. 89.

16. "Distinguished counsel": "Plan Assault," p. 5.

16. "John, we've been arguing": Scopes and Presley, *Center of the Storm*, p. 58.

18. "We have now learned": Hunter, *Civic Biology*, p. 194.

2. "WE'VE JUST ARRESTED A MAN FOR TEACHING EVOLUTION!"

21. "This is F. E. Robinson": Scopes and Presley, *Center of the Storm*, p. 60.

"I had been taught from childhood": Scopes and Presley, p. 4.

26. "Boy, I'm interested": Scopes and Presley, p. 63.

"keen and analytical mind": Scopes and Presley, p. 64.

"And whether you want": Scopes and Presley, p. 63.

"one of the warmest-hearted men.": Scopes and Presley, p. 63.

29. "the circus came to Dayton!": Scopes and Presley, p. 77.

31. "The Tennessee legislators who passed the law": "If Monkeys Could Speak."

3. MONKEYSHINES

33. "Man is descended": Darwin, *Descent*, p. 391.

34. "I keep all those things": Hague, "Reminiscence," p. 760.

35. "Although we know that man is separated": Hunter, *Civic Biology*, p. 195.

36. "If evolution wins, Christianity goes!": California State University, "Closing Statement."

"'Monkey' has become the most important": "Dayton Jolly," p. 1.

39. "wide-open bull sessions": Scopes and Presley, *Center of the Storm*, p. 40.

42. "I lapped it up": Linder, "Student Witnesses."

"The question is not": Shaub, "Bryan, 'Weak,'" p. 3.

43. "a model of the well-dressed man": Scopes and Presley, *Center of the Storm*, p. 91.

44. "down-in-the-mud fight": Scopes and Presley, p. 70.

46. "I know you!": Scopes and Presley, p. 86.

"With the arrival of Bryan": Scopes and Presley, p. 84.

47. "There never was anything else": Scopes and Presley, p. 84.

"They came in small automobiles": "Cranks and Freaks, p. 1.

48. "Christianity is strengthened by science": Moses, "Rev. W. H. Moses," p. 9.

"the greatest curse": Martin, *Hell and the High School*, p. 165.

49. "We're like moon men here": American Experience, "WGN Radio."

4. "DO YOU KNOW ANYTHING ABOUT EVOLUTION?"

57. "His huge head, leathery lined face": Larson, *Summer for the Gods*, p. 149.

"Here comes William": American Experience, "WGN Radio."

64. "the Holy Spirit may be with the jury": Horvath, *Transcript*, p. 1.

66. "Do you know anything about evolution?": Horvath, p. 51.

"Did you ever have any opinion?": Horvath, p. 52.

"I can't read!": Horvath, p. 18.

"Is that due to your eyes?": Horvath, p. 19.

"I preached against it, of course!": Horvath, p. 21.

"It was obvious": Mencken, *Religious Orgy*, p. 43.

68. "this Tennessee buffoonery": Mencken, p. 14.

"these forlorn backwaters": Mencken, p. 13.

"They are ignorant": Mencken, p. 12.

69. "Such obscenities as the forthcoming": Mencken, p. 11.

5. "THE FIRES THAT HAVE BEEN LIGHTED IN AMERICA"

71. "Be it enacted by the General Assembly": Horvath, *Transcript*, p. 101.

75. "Mr. Scopes might have taken his stand": Horvath, p. 118.

"If the state has a right in the exercise": Horvath, p. 126.

76. "Here we find today as brazen": Horvath, p. 129.

"I know there are millions": Horvath, p. 133.

77. "I will tell you what is going to happen": Horvath, p. 145.

"While he was talking": "Darrow Scores," p. 1.

78. "You have but a dim notion of it": Mencken, *Religious Orgy*, p. 61.

"Ignorance and fanaticism": Horvath, *Transcript*, p. 146.

6. "DID HE TELL YOU ANYTHING THAT WAS WICKED?"

82. "On that summer day": Scopes and Presley, *Center of the Storm*, p. 139.

"Where in the hell": Scopes and Presley, p. 139.

"A ringside observer": Scopes and Presley, p. 136.

"This fine mess I've gotten myself into": Linder, "John Scopes."

84. "A father just naturally": Linder.

87. "Go to the head of the class!": Horvath, *Transcript*, p. 207.

All of the quotes from the students' cross-examinations are from the Horvath, *Transcript*, pp. 207–13.

88. "It is for the mother of this boy to say": Moran, *Scopes Trial*, p. 106.

90. "Your Honor, every single word": Horvath, *Transcript*, p. 221.

92. "We shall show by the testimony": Horvath, p. 185.

"Will you state what evolution is": Horvath, p. 229.

"We except [object] to that!": Horvath, p. 229.

94. "Genesis is a much more": Larson, *Summer for the Gods*, p. 176.

"The floor on which we are now assembled": Horvath, *Transcript*, p. 276.

96. "How dared those scientists": Horvath, p. 284.

97. "We do not need any experts": Horvath, p. 293.

"The Christian believes": Horvath, p. 282.

"There is the book they were teaching": Horvath, p. 284.

"Tell me that the parents": Horvath, p. 284.

98. "If such people were lower": Hunter, *Civic Biology*, p. 263.

99. "Studies have been made": Hunter, p. 261.

100. "five races or varieties of man": Hunter, p. 196.

103. "I would like to say something": Horvath, *Transcript*, p. 302.

104. "The truth always wins": Horvath, p. 303.

"The truth is": Du Bois, *Crisis*, p. 218.

105. "duel to the death": Horvath, p. 277.

"And in the applauding": "Malone Meets Bryan."

"wholly irrelevant": Horvath, *Transcript*, p. 322.

106. "All that remains": Mencken, *Religious Orgy*, p. 89.

"It was as though the sportswriters": Scopes and Presley, *Center of the Storm*, p. 162.

8. "THE EVENING AND THE MORNING WERE THE FIRST DAY"

109. "Hell is going to pop now": Scopes and Presley, *Center of the Storm*, p. 165.

"The defense desires": Horvath, *Transcript,* p. 441.

"All of the lawyers": Scopes and Presley, *Center of the Storm*, p. 166.

110. "You have given considerable study": Horvath, *Transcript*, p. 442.

110–14. All of Darrow's cross-examination of Bryan is from Horvath, *Transcript*, pp. 442–77.

115. "It has brought about a striking revelation": "And Now for the Appeal," p. 10.

116. "I think, to save time": Horvath, *Transcript*, p. 480.

"Mr. Scopes, the jury has found": Horvath, p. 490.

117. "Your Honor, I feel that I have been": Horvath, p. 490.

118. "the indestructability": Horvath, p. 499.

118. "I was free of courtroom drama!": Scopes and Presley, *Center of the Storm*, p. 188.

9. THE CIRCUS LEAVES TOWN

119. "When a circus leaves town": Scopes and Presley, *Center of the Storm*, p. 191.

120. "Dayton was once": Scopes and Presley, p. 194.

"What happened": Scopes and Presley, p. 197.

122. "He fought the evolutionists": Larson, *Summer of Gods,* p. 204.

"Why, that man's got horns, I tell you!": Scopes and Presley, *Center of the Storm*, p. 200.

123. "Where one person had been interested": Cole, "50 Years Ago."

126. "find any text book on biology": Moore, "The Lingering Impact."

"wonderful discovery": Hunter, *Civic Biology*, p. 405.

"the great English scientist": Hunter, p. 194.

128. "We will bring chaos": Webb, *Evolution Controversy*, p. 146.

"I have no hope": Webb, p. 146.

EPILOGUE

133. "Your name has been": Scopes and Presley, *Center of the Storm*, p. 240.

133. "Notoriety is as tenacious": Scopes and Presley, p. 233.

"Monkey on my back": Scopes and Presley, p. 241.

134. "All humanity is descended": Bryan College, "About Bryan."

139. "I enjoyed the movie": Scopes and Presley, *Center of the Storm*, p. 270.

"The movie captured": Scopes and Presley, p. 270.

Image Credits

Alamy: 117

Photographs from the Bryan College Archive: 17, 37, 50, 56, 58, 59, 67 [bottom image], 75, 77, 84, 95, 118, 121

Courtesy of Anthony Elder: iv

Courtesy of the author: 96, 123

Getty Images: 49, 52, 65, 67 [top image], 135, 136–137

Library of Congress: 8, 13, 24, 33, 44, 101, 102

Public domain: 4, 9, 23, 34, 35, 69

Smithsonian Institution Archives: 6, 12, 14, 26, 54, 55, 91, 93, 108, 111

Bibliography

American Civil Liberties Union. "The Scopes Monkey Trial: A Look Back 85 Years Later." Fall 2009. www.acluohio.org/assets/issues/ReligiousLiberty /ScopesBooklet.pdf; accessed July 19, 2020.

American Experience, PBS. "WGN Radio Broadcasts the Trial." https://www.pbs.org/wgbh/americanexperience/ features/monkeytrial-wgn-radio-broadcasts-trial/; accessed February 13, 2021.

"And Now for the Appeal." *Baltimore Sun*, July 22, 1925.

"Arrest Under Evolution Law." *Nashville Banner*, May 6, 1925.

Blair, Mrs. E. P. "The Battle Hymn of Tennessee." *Nashville Tennessean*, June 29, 1925.

Bryan, William J. "W.G.N. Put 'On Carpet,' Gets a Bryan Lashing." *Chicago Tribune*, June 20, 1923.

Bryan College. "About Bryan." February 1, 2021. www .bryan.edu/about; accessed February 19, 2021.

California State University. "Text of the Closing Statement of William Jennings Bryan at the Trial of John Scopes." http://www2.csudh.edu/oliver/smt310-handouts/wjb-last/wjb-last.htm; accessed February 12, 2021.

Cohen, Andrew. "What the Scopes Trial Teaches Us About Climate Change Denial." *Atlantic*, October 1, 2013. https://www.theatlantic.com/national/archive/2013/10/what-the-scopes-trial-teaches-us-about-climate-change-denial/280098; accessed February 20, 2021.

Cole, Fay-Cooper. "50 Years Ago: A Witness at the Scopes Trial." *Scientific American*, December 31, 2008. www .scientificamerican.com/article/50-years-ago-scope-trial-witness; accessed July 12, 2020.

"Cranks and Freaks Flock to Dayton." *New York Times*, July 11, 1925.

Daly, Christopher. *Covering America: A Narrative History of a Nation's Journalism*. Amherst: University of Massachusetts Press, 2012.

Darrow, Clarence. "Darrow Asks Bryan to Answer These," *Chicago Tribune*, July 4, 1923.

———. *The Story of My Life*. New York: Da Capo Press, 1996. First published 1932.

"Darrow Scores." *New York Times*, July 14, 1925.

Darwin, Charles. *The Descent of Man*. New York: Penguin Press, 2004. First published in 1871.

———. *On the Origin of Species*. New York: Signet Classics Press, 2003. First published in 1859.

———. *The Voyage of the Beagle*. New York: Doubleday and Co., 1962. First published in 1839.

"Dayton Ape Battle Opens Today." *Roseburgh News Review*, July 10, 1925.

"Dayton Jolly as Evolution Trial Looms." *Chattanooga Times*, May 21, 1925.

Du Bois, W. E. B. "Scopes." *Crisis Magazine*: NAACP Newsletter, September 1925.

Farrell, John A. *Clarence Darrow: Attorney for the Damned*. New York: Random House, 2011.

Fundamentals, The: A Testimony. Chicago: Testimony Publishing Company, 1910.

Ginger, Ray. *Six Days or Forever: Tennessee v. John Thomas Scopes*. Oxford University Press, 1958.

Hague, James. "A Reminiscence of Mr. Darwin." *Harper's New Monthly Magazine* 69 (1884): 759–63, p. 760.

Historical Thinking Matters. "The Scopes Trial." historicalthinkingmatters.org/scopestrial; accessed June 1, 2020.

Hodge, Bodie. "How Old Is the Earth?" Answers In Genesis. May 30, 2007. answersingenesis.org/age-of-the-earth/how-old-is-the-earth; accessed June 3, 2020.

Horvath, Anthony, ed. *The Transcript of the Scopes Monkey Trial*. Greenwood, WI: Suzeteo Publishing, 2018.

Hunter, George William. *A Civic Biology: Presented in Problems*. New York: American Book Co., 1914.

"If Monkeys Could Speak." *Chicago Defender*. May 23, 1925.

Kazin, Michael. *A Godly Hero: The Life of William Jennings Bryan*. New York: Anchor Books, 2007.

LaFollette, Marcel. *Reframing Scopes: Journalists, Scientists and Lost Photographs from the Trial of the Century*. Lawrence: University Press of Kansas, 2008.

Larson, Edward. *Summer for the Gods: The Scopes Trial and America's Continuing Debate Over Science and Religion*. Cambridge, MA: Basic Books, 1997.

Linder, Douglas O. "John Scopes." University of Missouri-Kansas City School of Law. 2004. law2.umkc .edu/faculty/projects/ftrials/scopes/Sco_sco.htm; accessed February 17, 2021.

———. "The Student Witnesses in the Scopes Trial." University of Missouri-Kansas City School of Law. 2004. famous-trials.com/scopesmonkey/2394-the-student -witnesses-in-the-scopes-trial; accessed February 17, 2021.

Losh, William J. "Scientific Evidence Ruled Out by Judge in Evolution Case." *Brooklyn Times,* July 17, 1925.

"Malone Meets Bryan," *Chattanooga Daily Times,* July 17, 1925.

Martin, T. T. *Hell and the High School.* Kansas City, MO: Western Baptist Publishing Co., 1923.

Mencken, H. L. "Darrow's Eloquent Appeal Wasted on Ears That Hear Only Bryan." *Baltimore Evening Sun,* July 14, 1925.

———. "Homo Neanderthalensis." *Baltimore Evening Sun,* June 29, 1925.

———. *A Religious Orgy in Tennessee: A Reporter's Account of the Scopes Monkey Trial.* Brooklyn, NY: Melville House Publishing, 2006.

"Monkey Trial Scopes Offered $150,000." *Chattanooga Times,* June 18, 1925.

Moore, Randy. "The Lingering Impact of the Scopes Trial on High School Biology Textbooks." *BioScience* 51, no. 9 (September 2001): 790–96. https://academic.oup.com/ bioscience/article/51/9/790/288261; accessed Nov. 23, 2020.

Moran, Jeffrey P. *American Genesis: The Evolution Controversies from Scopes to Creation Science.* Oxford University Press, 2012.

———. *The Scopes Trial: A Brief History with Documents.* Boston: Bedford/St. Martins, 2002.

Moses, W. H. "Rev. W. H. Moses, Attending Evolution Trial, States Reaction Will Favor Race." *Pittsburgh Courier,* July 25, 1925.

"Plan Assault." *Chattanooga Times,* May 4, 1925.

Quammen, David. *The Reluctant Mr. Darwin: An Intimate Portrait of Charles Darwin and the Making of His Theory of Evolution*. New York: W. W. Norton and Co., 2007.

"Riled by Mencken Slurs, Dayton Citizens Want to Put Him Out." *Pittsburgh Gazette Times*, July 17, 1925.

Sands, Kathleen. *America's Religious Wars: The Embattled Heart of Our Public Life*. New Haven, CT: Yale University Press, 2019.

Scopes, John T., and James Presley. *Center of the Storm: Memoirs of John T. Scopes*. New York: Holt, Rinehart and Winston, 1967.

Shaub, Earl. "Bryan, 'Weak in Knees,' Fires Shots at Theory of Evolution." *El Paso Times*, May 19, 1925.

Szalay, Jessie. "Scopes Monkey Trial: Science on the Stand. *Live Science*. October 1, 2016. www.livescience.com/56343-scopes-monkey-trial.html; accessed June 30, 2020.

"A Venerable Orang-Outang: A Contribution to Unnatural History." *Hornet*, March 22, 1871.

Webb, George. *The Evolution Controversy in America*. Lexington: University Press of Kentucky, 1994.

Resources for Young Readers

Historical Thinking Matters. "The Scopes Trial."
historicalthinkingmatters.org/scopestrial

A website focused on U.S. history, designed by Stanford University and George Mason University. Uses primary sources to help students examine historical events critically.

The Devil on Trial: Witches, Anarchists, Atheists, Communists, and Terrorists in America's Courtrooms by Phillip Margulies and Maxine Rosaler (Houghton Mifflin Harcourt, 2008)

A nonfiction account of the Scopes trial and other famous, thought-provoking trials.

Monkey Town: The Summer of the Scopes Trial by Ronald Kidd (Simon and Schuster, 2006)

A middle grade novel that captures the atmosphere and personalities of Dayton in July 1925.

Index

Page numbers in *italics* indicate illustrations.